To Anita

Backstage
with Jeanette

Warmest Wishes
Jeanette

Backstage
with Jeanette

Jeanette Wilson

RANDOM HOUSE
NEW ZEALAND

National Library of New Zealand Cataloguing-in-Publication Data
Wilson, Jeanette, 1962-
Backstage with Jeanette Wilson / Jeanette Wilson.
ISBN 978-1-86941-893-9
1. Wilson, Jeanette, 1962- 2. Women mediums—New Zealand.
3. Psychic ability. 4. Spiritualism. I. Title.
133.91—dc 22

A RANDOM HOUSE BOOK
published by
Random House New Zealand
18 Poland Road, Glenfield, Auckland, New Zealand
www.randomhouse.co.nz

Random House International
Random House
20 Vauxhall Bridge Road
London, SW1V 2SA
United Kingdom

Random House Australia (Pty) Ltd
20 Alfred Street, Milsons Point, Sydney,
New South Wales 2061, Australia

Random House South Africa Pty Ltd
Isle of Houghton
Corner Boundary Road and Carse O'Gowrie
Houghton 2198, South Africa

Random House Publishers India Private Ltd
301 World Trade Tower, Hotel Intercontinental Grand Complex,
Barakhamba Lane, New Delhi 110 001, India

First published 2007

© 2007 Jeanette Wilson

The moral rights of the author have been asserted

ISBN 978 1 86941 893 9

This book is copyright. Except for the purposes of fair reviewing no part of this publication may be reproduced or transmitted in any form or by any means, electronic or mechanical, including photocopying, recording or any information storage and retrieval system, without permission in writing from the publisher.

Text and cover design: Katy Yiakmis
Cover photo: Chris Coad
Printed in Australia by Griffin Press

Contents

Introduction 7
1. After the Show 13
2. Finding Resolution and Closure 34
3. Helping Ourselves and Others to Grieve 48
4. Murders and Missing People 65
5. Spirits that Don't Rest 79
6. Losing a Child 95
7. Why Do Spirits Communicate with Us? 111
8. A New Perspective on Suicide 128
9. Forgiveness 143
10. Helping People to Die 164
11. Something More to Life 184
12. Children and Spirits 201
Appendix 222

Introduction

At the end of each show there are always those who wait patiently to see me. They often wait for an hour or more, sometimes supported by a friend, sometimes sitting it out alone as the queue for signed books disappears and the hands on the clock move slowly forward. I am aware of them and of their loved ones who have passed over as I answer the questions of the audience and sign their books.

The ones who *really* need to see me always wait. They overcome that little voice of the ego that tells them not to be so needy, not to trouble me when I am already tired. I always say that after the show has finished I will not do any more mediumship. It is true, for I am too tired. But, every now and then, spirit world has a different idea and I find myself sitting with a complete stranger in the wee hours, opening myself once more to the spiritual dimensions to see what it is their loved ones who have passed over have to say.

Somehow, though it always baffles me quite how, there is always the time and the energy to make these last and very vital connections. The stage show sometimes seems to be a warm-up for these most poignant and beautiful messages of the evening. They are messages that invariably have meaning for us all, but the sensitive circumstances around them mean that they cannot be recorded for television or even delivered in front of an audience. Even writing about them here I have had to be especially careful to ensure that none could be identified, except by their nearest and dearest, as I would not wish to add to the pain of those concerned.

In this book I share with you the most significant of these messages, described in a way that their essence remains but the details are sufficiently changed to prevent identification of individuals. Sometimes I have blended the insights received from a number of loved ones who have passed away, while retaining the integrity of each communication. I also share with you more about the kind of things that happen when I am not on stage.

The mediumship shows that you see on your television screens are a small but important part of what I do. As Spirit told me years ago, my work here is *to give people proof*. Proof that their loved ones haven't died, proof that we are more than we believe ourselves to be, and proof that there is more to this world. It's a role that takes me into many areas: searching for loved ones who are missing or believed to have died, helping people to heal, helping people to die, helping others to live better and more fulfilling lives. It's a role that I love. I sometimes think I have more beautiful moments than anyone else I know, but I also get to feel a lot of pain, other people's pain, and so at times the task is a bitter-sweet one.

I have learned now not to resist the pain, to simply allow it. Life has its good moments and its bad and the secret seems to be to feel whatever is happening fully, to be open to it. When you are open to this moment you are open to life. And when we are open to life the healing begins. We start to feel the connectedness that deep down we all crave — with each other and with God.

Life has taught me much. I have learned that all of us have been hurt in some way by what we have been through in this lifetime. All of us have felt fear or despair at some stage in our lives. Some of us clearly have had more pain than others, and more difficult obstacles to overcome, and you will find some of their stories on these pages.

Stories can help us to understand, and real life stories can help us to understand about real life. We don't all need to go through what some of the people on the pages of this book have been through, but we can learn from their experiences. We can take time to imagine what it must have been like for them and we can feel compassion and love for them as they continue on their journey, and also for the family they leave behind. In doing so, we help them and their families to heal and we also help ourselves move forward through our own pain and into a new level of understanding.

Compassion is a soul energy. It is love expressed as desire for another to be free of suffering. Our journey here is an individual one but it is helped enormously by the love and compassion of others. All of the people referred to in this book are getting through their pain and moving on with their lives, assisted by the love and compassion of those around them, the seen and the unseen. They still miss their loved ones dearly, but the pain of separation is diminished as they have each, in their own way, come to realise that death is an illusion and that love is eternal.

I hope that the stories you read in this book give you comfort and help you to move forward in your own way, whatever that may be. I hope that between the pages of this book you find some answers and also some questions, for the more we question, the more we come to understand, and the more we come to understand, the more we feel at peace — with ourselves and with each other.

To those whose pain
is greatest & whose
love is deepest

1. After the Show

I was at a complete loss for words and time seemed to stand still. I could feel my stomach tightening as a pair of female eyes implored me to say the right thing: not just 'right' in saying what they wanted me to say, but to tell them the truth.

I felt like my brain had frozen. Whatever could anyone say to make this one 'all right'?

The theatre foyer, which had been a buzz of excited activity moments before, was now empty apart from myself and the lady in front of me. She was well-dressed and in her mid-fifties. Her rounded face showed she was a kindly soul who had seen her fair share of life. She struck me as a lady who would do no harm; one who genuinely cared for others. In lots of ways she was like many women I have met over the years, but I could also sense that she was different. This lady held a pain, a deep pain, one that few would ever comprehend, let alone experience.

Evelyn had stayed to see me at the end of the show because we both knew that her pain was one that could not be safely explored in front of a public audience. She had waited patiently for over an hour as I had signed books, answered questions and given a couple of healings that I was guided to do. It was well after 11 pm by the time she got to speak to me in private; the theatre staff had all but closed down the theatre and were getting ready to leave. I could see that Evelyn was oblivious to their impatience — right now she had something else far more important on her mind.

Evelyn's hazel eyes were unflinching in their intensity. I could feel her gaze almost burrowing into me. I felt that she thought that somehow if she went into my head she would see what I saw and get the answers she so badly needed.

Evelyn desperately wanted to know if I had a message for her.

I took my awareness out of her desperation and into the spiritual dimensions. I could see immediately that she had two children in spirit world. The eldest, a young man, came through first and strongest. He had passed over not long ago — just a few years. His death had been a huge shock. I knew that he had been involved in a road accident.

He was so sorry for leaving her. Remorse flowed through me. Evelyn had loved him and continued to love him *so much*. He had always known that love was there for him and that felt so good for him while he was here, and continued to serve him well in spirit world.

'His hair is so messy!' I exclaimed. In my head I couldn't take my eyes off his hair — it looked like dreadlocks. 'You couldn't get a comb through it.'

Then the dam burst — Evelyn was sobbing. Instinctively I knew she could sense her son with me and for the first time she knew that he was all right. The relief was almost tangible.

'That's him!' She smiled when she was at last able to compose herself. 'You really couldn't get a comb through it,' she said, shaking her head.

Matt, her son, was just the same as he had been here. We talked for a little while about what he was experiencing in spirit world and the events leading up to his passing. As much as Matt was communicating with her, I could sense that there was still something more Evelyn needed, something else she needed to ask.

Then I saw her. A young girl in spirit world was circling me excitedly.

'Matt is showing me a beautiful young girl in spirit world. She is running around me at waist height. There is so much joy. Her fun-filled eyes are laughing at me as if to say "Look at me, look at what I can do, I can run circles around you." '

The little girl I was seeing was so full of life, but somehow I *knew* her little feet had never walked this earth, and that she had left this physical realm as a baby. Before I had a chance to convert what I was perceiving into words, the question Evelyn had been holding onto burst out.

She was in tears again, her voice breaking as she spoke. 'Was he taken because of what I did?'

Inside I knew that Evelyn had made the decision to terminate her daughter when she was in the womb. I was speechless, and yet out of my mouth came a very assured voice. 'No, you absolutely did the right thing, I would stake my life on it.'

I usually sit very firmly on the fence with matters such as terminations as there are so many angles that we may not see — so the words coming out of my mouth took me completely by surprise. I would stake my life on it!? Why such a strong opinion and where had it come from? Why was it the 'right' choice? I was feeling a little uncomfortable and hoping that whoever was talking through me would back up what they were saying with some hard evidence.

The words had just tripped out of my mouth — now I wanted an explanation. There were lots of questions in my head, not least of which was how come it was so clear-cut that it was the 'right' thing to do. I wasn't getting any answers and so I put the questions to one side for a moment while I gave Evelyn my full attention once more.

'I terminated her before birth,' Evelyn confessed. Her voice was little more than a whisper as she spoke. 'The doctors told me there was no choice. She would have had severe Down's syndrome. They did all the tests.'

I found myself holding Evelyn, like a mother comforts a child. I wished that she could wake up from this nightmare, be free of it. She was having to live with it every day of her life.

It was then that she looked up at me and asked the question I simply couldn't answer: 'Was Matt taken as a punishment for what I did?'

I knew that was the real question, the one that kept her awake at night, the one that didn't let her spirit rest.

And that is when time stood still. I was in the scene being played out before my eyes but not of it. It wasn't the more usual shock, fear or denial that had taken me into this state, it was a calming energy that simply came over me and caused me to be still.

In the stillness I found that I didn't have to think to find the answer. Amy, the beautiful baby girl that she terminated, was with me in my body now and this delightful six-year-old responded wonderfully, better than I ever could. She spoke through me gently, reassuringly, without a trace of doubt. Her words moved us both deeply:

'Mum, when you made the decision to stop my birth, my consciousness was with you in your head and your body. The decision for me not to be born into the physical world was one we made together. *It was a shared decision.*' She slowly emphasised the last sentence.

All the doubt and all the guilt Evelyn had felt over the past thirty years was washed away with that one simple insight. It was not a concept that had ever entered my consciousness before, and it brought huge relief. Evelyn had lived with the worry of not knowing if she had made the right decision ever since the termination. Then, when her son Matt died so tragically, she started to question if that was some kind of punishment from God. She had wondered if somehow in terminating her daughter she had not valued life and so God was teaching her its value.

Now her beautiful daughter had given her another perspective — one that was a lot less painful to hold.

Life had given Evelyn and Amy the opportunity of knowing, through the amniocentesis test, that Amy had Down's syndrome and would be severely handicapped. There had been no doubt about this. At the point the decision was made there were two consciousnesses in Evelyn: her own and her unborn daughter's, and the decision to terminate was one they made together. The soul of the incarnating child could see that a physical incarnation was just going to be too hard and not what it wanted.

I was a little in shock, as I had never considered

terminations in that way before. Now I thought about it, it made perfect sense. Such a simple insight and yet so liberating for Evelyn.

Here on a physical level we see life mainly through our physical eyes and we sometimes debate the value of a handicapped life. Yes, absolutely, all life is of value; we all have access to the same divine power within us and around us. All lives are equal, although not all will be born into equal opportunities or have apparently equal qualities. Nevertheless all life is equal because we all have equal opportunities to learn and to grow, and to know God. It is just that our souls are at different levels of evolution and make different choices.

On this occasion though, all of that was immaterial because it was the choice of the incarnating soul not to complete the birth process.

Wow! I was in awe of the wisdom of this effervescent six-year-old girl still running circles around me. Once again the value of communicating with those who have passed on was shaking the foundations of my own beliefs. Once again, spirit world was giving a new and more empowering perspective on a life situation: one that washed away Evelyn's misplaced guilt and dissolved her pain of not knowing.

Although Amy would have been in her thirties had she lived, she appeared to me as a child, for this was what Mum missed. Evelyn had missed the experience of bringing up a girl — instead she had

had three boys. In coming through as a child Amy was letting Mum know that she hadn't missed out on being 'Mum' to her. Amy would be waiting for her as a little girl when the time came. That was what Mum wanted.

For now it was time to hug once more. Amy was in my body embracing Mum in a way only six-year-old girls know how. I knew I couldn't bring Matt or Amy back but at least there would not now be the same level of suffering; the mental torture of not knowing if she was to blame. It would take more time but eventually there could be resolution and peace. Evelyn had taken a big step forward and we all knew it. Matt and Amy were very happy.

After Evelyn and I had said our goodbyes my thoughts turned to terminations generally and about how the spirit or soul comes into the physical form. I knew from my own experience that my daughter Sarah's spirit had been with me from conception. I also felt that more of the spirit then came in at birth and thereafter. I hold the view that we have basically three parts to us: our physical personality self (who we think we are); our individuated soul or spirit (some would say holy spirit); and that part of us that knows that we are all one, all part of God. For ease of reference I will refer to the part of us that is individuated as Spirit and the part that knows itself as One/God as the soul (the sole or only one). Some writers may use the words the other way around, describing the individuated soul as 'soul' and describing the Oneness/God as Great Spirit. Either way is acceptable.

From my experience with my own children and other people's babies I have reached the conclusion that children are born into this world open, feeling connected to all, aware of oneness. Life experiences can then close down their ability to truly feel and stop them from experiencing the pure joy of simply being alive.

In the days that followed my meeting with Evelyn I found myself being reminded about the beliefs of Rudolf Steiner, the Austrian head of the Theosophical Society in Germany and the founder of the Anthroposophical Society. At the risk of greatly over-simplifying the work of these two organisations, the Theosophical Society is involved with the study of spirituality ('theo' means God in Greek) and the Anthroposophical Society is about studying humanity ('anthropos' means man in Greek). Rudolf Steiner is perhaps best known for his legacy of Steiner/Waldorf schools, and he made significant contributions to the development and promotion of bio-dynamic agriculture.

Rudolf Steiner believed that we are each composed of body, spirit and soul. Waldorf schools reflect Steiner's education theories, which hold that children advance through three stages and that education should be appropriate to the spirit for each stage. During the first stage, birth to age seven, the spirit inhabiting the body of the child is still adjusting to its surroundings, hence lower grades in Waldorf schools offer minimal academic content. Reading is not introduced until second or third grade. During the second stage, ages seven to fourteen, children are said to be driven primarily by imagination and fantasy, so students are introduced to mythology.

I have been drawn to the work of Rudolf Steiner over the years and his beliefs have influenced the development of the Eco School (www.ecoschool.co.nz), though the Eco School is not affiliated in any way with any Steiner/Waldorf organisations. It is this school that my own children attend when we are not travelling.

I had no way of knowing if Rudolf Steiner's beliefs were correct. All I knew was that as my children grew older more of who they were, their spirit, seemed to be coming through. Perhaps that's why the teenage years can be particularly difficult for some children, and their parents. I hadn't been aware of any big shifts though, apart from at birth. The process had seemed a lot more gradual to me.

I also recognised that there had been moments, profound moments, when each of my children had spoken to myself, my partner Andrew and others with pure wisdom way beyond their physical years.

Each of my children have at different times cupped Daddy's face in their small hands, looked straight into his eyes and asked, 'Daddy, why aren't you doing what you want with your life?' For a silent few moments both Daddy (Andrew) and I were very aware that it was not our child, who we thought of as Liam or Sarah, in that small body. Someone else, or a higher aspect of them, was talking through them and asking what needed to be asked.

Sarah asked that question at three years of age, and Liam did exactly the same thing a few years later, when he was four. And no, Daddy still isn't doing what he wants to with his life, but there are the signs that this is starting to change.

Our children have each come out with statements that are both profoundly simple and incredibly wise.

'Do you know, Mummy, I can never have this day again,' said a smiling Sarah as we came home from school one day. I am sure she didn't know just how significant this was. In her own words she was encapsulating the wisdom of the Greek philosopher Heraclitus, who said: 'You cannot step twice into the same river, for other waters are continually flowing in.' She was appreciating that life was a flow, that she too was changing and that she could indeed never have this day again. She was recognising that she needed to make the most of and enjoy each day — and she does. Andrew and I both learn so much from her and her brother Liam.

At school every now and then a pearl of wisdom

will fall out of one of their mouths. This story was recounted to me by one of Sarah's teachers. The class was making 'memory mats', weaving strands of paper together in much the same way as you would weave flax. Each piece of paper was a different colour and the children identified what each of the colours meant to them, using their memory.

As one child took a strip of pale blue paper to weave into their map they explained that the pale blue to them was sadness. Another child immediately said, 'I don't want any of that in my mat.' Sarah reached across and took some pale blue too. As Sarah wove the pale blue strand of paper into her mat she said, 'I am glad we have sadness, because without sadness we wouldn't know what happiness was.' She was just six years old. Most grown-ups haven't learned to appreciate sadness yet, including myself at times. We resist it. We don't like feeling it. We would rather it was not there. Imagine how different your life would be if you could appreciate sadness, see it for what it was, a feeling moving through you that adds to the rich tapestry of life and to the precious feeling of being 'alive'.

Over the years I have heard many such stories about other 'inspired' children saying and doing similar things that stop us adults in our tracks. My children are not that unusual. Little incidents like these are happening all the time — we just need to notice them more.

Each of these stories is good evidence to me that within the child there is not only learned information but also a storehouse of wisdom waiting to be tapped into. And that is the reason we need to refine the way we are educating our children.

The word 'educate' comes from the Latin word 'educare' or 'educe' which means to draw out from within. Interesting then that if we look up the word 'educate' in a modern dictionary we read that it means to develop the faculties and powers of a person by teaching, instruction or schooling. Synonyms are: instruct, school, drill, indoctrinate. Could this be where our education system is going wrong? Children who don't respond well to being filled with facts, or who can't file facts in memory in a way suitable for retrieval in exam conditions, are written off as 'dumb', when in lots of other ways they are clearly very intelligent. Is it any wonder our youth get cross when the education system, and we, as the society that supports that education system, fail them?

Some of the better teachers are undoubtedly working with their pupils to help them find out who they are and what they are capable of doing and are getting good results, but how much better it would be if the system recognised the child's inner wisdom in some way. The child would learn to value him- or herself and to think, feel and reason for themselves. Some children are doing this already but it tends to be despite the education system, not because of it.

Our eyes may tell us that the child is very young in physical years, but remember the spirit within is eternal and has lived many previous incarnations. Even though the child may be very young, even so young as to be still in the womb, the divine intelligence of the spirit is still there and can guide us if we allow it.

Was it possible then, I wondered, that for each decision made about terminating a pregnancy, the spirit of the incarnating child was party to that decision? Instead of it being Mum and Dad making the decision, was it the presence of the spirit of the unborn child influencing and guiding the parents? If it was, wouldn't it make all such decisions easier to live with?

And what about miscarriages? Did it mean that it was the incarnating spirit just deciding not to incarnate after all? Could the mother's physical body be affected and cause her to lose a child even if Mum herself really wanted that child? Yes, it seemed it could. The incarnating child has free will and if it does not want to stay here, no one — not even Mum — can keep it here.

That brought me to another question. Was it possible, then, that a person could not leave this place without it being their own free choice? That was an entirely bigger question and I realised I was opening up a great big can of worms. I could feel myself struggling with the enormity of it. I had to still myself and become very quiet to listen to the response from one of my guides.

'When we understand who we are, we will no longer fear death. For death is but a transition from this dimension into the next. All that we experience here is experienced through choice. Our free will. Do you think that your free will is taken away from you at some stage? All we experience here is a result of our free-will choices.'

Now my head was spinning and my heart was pounding.

'But what about murders?' I asked my guide internally. 'What about children that die young? Was that their choice?'

'Here (meaning the physical dimension) it is sometimes difficult to see the underlying causes for the events that unfold, but we assure you that nothing here can happen against a person's free will.'

I could find myself getting agitated.

'What about rapes? What about robberies? Are you telling me that the victims of such crimes chose to experience these things?'

'Yes. Your time on the earth is a time of experiencing the different qualities of the heart (an anagram of earth). The heart centre is where the physical energies are combined with the higher spiritual frequencies. Here your task is to operate through the heart, transmuting the lower vibrational energies, such as fear and anxiety, into more loving positive energies.'

'I get that,' I said, 'but why on earth would anyone ever choose to be raped or murdered, or to die in a fire?'

'As you journey through life you come to understand yourself, your thoughts and feelings, your likes and dislikes. You come to recognise that you have feelings and that these feelings, as well as your thoughts, ripple out and affect your reality. You know this. You have observed this in your own life and in the lives of others. Do you really think that there are exceptions to the law of cause and effect? Do you really think there is some other more powerful force, either good or bad, that comes in and causes you to have different experiences from the ones you are creating for yourself through your choices?'

I was dumbfounded. It was logical. The teaching continued.

'There is no one here more powerful than you; you hold all the power when you are conscious in this moment. Every thought you have ever had makes a difference, every feeling you have ever felt makes a difference.'

'I still don't feel you have answered my question,' I protested. I was confused and badly needed clarity. 'Why would a person choose murder, for example?'

'Certainly there may not be a conscious choice made through the mind — "I want to be murdered"

— the choice is for the most part an unconscious one, although aspects of it may be revealed to the conscious mind through dreams.'

'Do you mean like a premonition?'

'Yes. Except it is not a premonition in the commonly understood sense. It is not some divine intelligence giving you a warning of what is to come. It is your subconscious mind bringing into your conscious mind that which you are already creating at some level. At some level the person is always ready to leave this plane.'

I found myself struggling with the concept. 'I can accept that, but I can't accept that someone would choose murder. It doesn't make sense.'

I was feeling really frustrated inside, but the voice talking to me continued softly and patiently.

'This experience of life is not just about having all the things your ego wants and desires, it is about the evolution of your soul. Learning to feel, to love, to care, to feel your connection with the whole of life. The soul chooses the experiences it needs to return to its sense of wholeness/Oneness. In some cases the soul wishes to learn forgiveness, to feel compassion for another and what they have been through. In others the soul is choosing what it is like to be brave, to have experiences that will help them find their inner strength and their inner connection. The reasons that things happen in this dimension are many and varied. Causes of circumstances can sometimes be hard to distinguish from a physical viewpoint, but cause and effect is a physical law — all effects have a cause.'

I had another question: 'Is it possible someone here could have lots of negative thoughts and somehow cause themselves a horrible death?'

The voice continued. 'Possible but very unlikely. They would have to think very negative thoughts over a prolonged time and often those around them would be aware of this and take steps to get them the help they needed. This not about the death being caused by mind on a physical level, this is about the spirit's journey, what the soul has chosen to experience.'

'If I were to say this to someone whose child had been murdered, I don't think it would go down very well,' I responded.

'No, probably not, but that doesn't stop it from being true. We each hold all potentials within us and all the choices we make here, be they conscious choices or unconscious ones, cause us to have the experiences we have.'

The questions in my head were still coming. 'But how does this help a family who has lost someone find resolution or closure?' Still my guide was patient with me, completely unaffected by my frustration.

'Resolution only comes when the person goes within and feels their unresolved feelings. Completion only comes when their mind lets the matter go.'

'I am now feeling really frustrated. I really want

to understand what you are saying but don't see how this is going to help people.'

The peacefulness of my guide within contrasted so strongly with my screeching question, that it took me by surprise. I wasn't sure if my guide was becoming more peaceful in response to my increasing level of unrest, or if it was maintaining the same peaceful quality and my increasing frustration made my guide now appear so peaceful to me.

'Everything that happens to us in life is feedback. Nothing needs to be taken personally. What is, just is. As you notice the reactions within you, you see what it is that you are holding that is keeping you from peace. Keeping you from experiencing Oneness with All. Even now, listening to my words, there is resistance within you — why? You want to help people release their pain, you want to "fix" them. You want to give them the words and the insights that will make everything okay. But perhaps what they are experiencing is exactly as it should be. Perhaps their life experience, the loss of that partner or child is bringing up their pain, their fear of loss, their fear of death, their fear of separation so they can see it for what it is and let it go.'

'Why does it have to be so hard?' I asked. My own journey had not been that painful but I had met others who had been through so much and still carried so much pain.

'It doesn't.' The words were said compassionately, reassuringly. 'If you can see life for what it is, and not take what happens personally, you will be open to it.'

'Open to death and suffering?' I could feel myself becoming cynical.

'Yes,' the voice was so patient with me, 'and open to life in all its magnificence.'

My frustration had fallen away. I didn't understand why, whether it was the words or the way they were said, but something had caused me to let it all go. I still didn't understand.

'I don't think you have answered my question about why things like murders happen.'

'Perhaps the real question is "Why do you react the way you do to murders?"'

The penny dropped. I was still inside again.

It isn't about *why* things happen, it's about how I *feel* about the things that happen. All of that teaches me about me; all of that helps me move forward. As Spirit we are eternal and so our journey is an eternal one. It is like a circle that never ends. It doesn't matter where we are on the circle — what matters is that we keep moving. Life happens and we react. Do we react through fear or through love? Do we react from our limited sense of self (our ego) or from deep within (our soul)? Do we trust life — or do we fear it? Are we open to all our experiences here or do we shy away from those we somehow consider 'negative'? Do we trust that we are in safe hands or do we buy into the concept of death and suffering that our minds create?

Our spirits are eternal. We will never, ever die. Life is an opportunity for us to express the gifts of our soul through this physical body. It's an opportunity we should make the most of. How we die is determined by our soul, for the lessons it has chosen.

Through the eyes of our physical self we may never know why a loved one left this plane in the way that they did, but we can have faith and trust that whatever we experience here will help us each become more loving, more compassionate and caring souls.

*Often the most beautiful people we know
have known pain and suffering and loss.
And they have come through it.
Often it is through such experiences that we
come to understand life better.
Life teaches us to develop compassion,
gentleness and a loving concern for others . . .
If we let it.
Beautiful people remind us that we are
God's Work in progress.*

2. Finding Resolution and Closure

I first saw him in a dream. He was tall, lanky I guess you would call him, in army camouflage fatigues. I saw him writing a note. He didn't want to do it. He didn't really want to end his life; it had been a cry for help. I only saw him briefly but my connection with him was so strong, it was as though I was with him in the room, watching everything, feeling all that he felt.

As I awoke I lay still for a while trying to recall as much of the dream as I could. I wondered if the young man I had seen was somehow linked with the lady I had spoken to on the phone the day before. Anthea had somehow managed to phone me on my home number (and believe you me it is not a number

I give out freely). She had lost a son quite recently. She told me that he had taken his own life in the UK and that a family member had to bring his body home. Was it him I had dreamed of? Or had I just tuned into someone else who was leaving the earth plane? Time would tell.

In *really* exceptional circumstances I see people privately. I never charge for this work, but simply make myself available to those with the greatest need. I know who I need to see and when, and in a way I am really glad it works like that. If I had to decide which people to see and which not I don't think I could. How do you gauge whose pain is greatest? Or which spirits most need to come through? I would end up seeing everyone and there would be no time for anything else, for my family, for the books or for my own personal development work.

Thankfully I don't get to choose and I am immensely grateful for that. The hard part though is communicating the decision when I decline a request. I still find that difficult and expect that I probably always will.

Hearing this particular lady's voice on the phone I had instinctively known that she was one I needed to see. I made an appointment with her for the end of the month. It was a couple of weeks before the appointment came around and that morning as I noticed her name in my diary my thoughts flashed back to the dream. Was that my mind? Or was it the spirit presence of the son? I wasn't sure, so I let all thoughts go and got on with the work ahead of me.

In the evening Anthea rang me. Where was I? Had I forgotten their appointment? I felt dreadful. I knew she had arranged for the rest of the family to be there. They must have all sat around waiting, waiting, getting more and more emotional, not knowing if I was on my way or why I wasn't there. And I had simply forgotten.

It didn't make sense. How could I have forgotten? The appointment was in my diary as clearly as anything. I had even noticed it that morning. Instead of keeping the appointment I picked the kids up from school, took them swimming and then we all went to Nana's to show her the kids' first swimming certificates.

The appointment had slipped my mind completely. Why? I never miss appointments. Never? Okay, so I did once miss a birthday party the kids were supposed to go to — but that apart I always remember appointments because I am good at writing things in my diary: it is a learned behaviour. If the appointment had not been in my diary I could have understood it, but it was. If I had not looked in my diary that day, again I could have understood it, but that didn't apply either. Why?

It wasn't until the next day that I would find out. Until then I was in sackcloth and ashes mode. I was mortified that I could forget something so important.

What must the family be going through? And why hadn't Spirit alerted me?

I had no excuse and as much as I apologised to Anthea on the phone I knew that an apology just doesn't cut it in such situations. I suggested seeing the family the next day at the same time. Unfortunately, this meant not all the family could be there as they could not take more time off work.

I felt so bad about the whole situation that I got Andrew to drive me to their home the next day. It was just as well he did. Going up the drive to the house I had a young male spirit take over my body. This time I was in absolutely no doubt that it was Anthea's young son who was with me.

I was 'shit-scared' — not language I think I have ever used in my life. I was absolutely dreading facing the family. I knew I had been dreading seeing them in a way because of the missed appointment, but this was different; now it was ten times worse. My heart was racing and my palms were sweating and I knew I hadn't been like this a few minutes before. I recognised that this wasn't my fear, this was the son's. He was scared but his resolve was strong; this was something he had to do. He wasn't going to back out, not now.

I recognised his photo as soon as we went into the lounge. His hair had been shorter than in the photo but I knew it was him. The photo showed him in happier times.

I settled myself on the sofa and in no time at all

Cole was talking through me. He was sorry, really really sorry. He felt such a fool — his family confirmed this was just how he was talking in the days leading up to his death. A chemical had tipped him off balance. He had been down and had taken a small white pill that he thought would help him feel better, but it didn't, it made him feel worse, much, much worse.

Cole had wanted someone to find him and for his girlfriend to understand just how much he cared. Cole's sister confirmed that Cole had taken his own life just a few steps away from others. No one had walked in on him. They could have done but they didn't. Not until it was too late.

'Rope.' It was out of my mouth before I had time to think. I could see a hangman's rope dangling from his photograph. Part of me wished I hadn't said it. It was so brutal, but Mum just nodded knowingly. Her son had hanged himself. Thankfully, Cole didn't dwell on it: he was conveying to me that there was another photograph — one that he preferred. Mum confirmed that she was getting a different picture of him enlarged, one she really liked and which had been Cole's favourite.

'She wasn't worth it,' he sobbed. He could see that now, but it was too late.

Cole's presence was moving my fingers. 'Fingers, fingers.'

He was telling me that there was a ring. There was and it had been returned to the family.

He hadn't wanted to die. It had been a gesture, designed to get a reaction. He hadn't meant for it to be so final. Now he felt like an even bigger fool because she was *so* not worth it.

On the spiritual side of life Cole had seen all the pain his actions had caused and he had come to understand what real love was. He had felt the love of his family, a love that had been there for him all along, but he just hadn't been able to see it at that time.

He drew my attention to the 'shite' note he had left. He really wished he hadn't left that note. In my mind I saw him tearing it up. Then it clicked — this was what the very first dream had been about: he didn't want to do it, as in take his own life, and he didn't want to — write such an awful note. It was him I had seen.

I was shown that Cole now knew that his lifetime had been one of learning the hard way that we have to accept responsibility for our actions. It was his lesson in life and his lesson in death.

Time after time in physical life Cole had made decisions that had consequences. Some of these decisions had really affected those he loved in a negative way. By taking his own life he had again made a choice that hurt those he loved. He was so sorry for everything, but at last he was beginning to understand that his words, thoughts, actions and feelings had consequences and that he was responsible for them. It had been a hard lesson and he had done it the hard way — as he tended to do in life.

Cole explained that as he died he had let go of all that he thought was important. 'You see everything for how it really was, not how you thought it was.'

In that split second he would not have chosen to die but the realisation had come too late — the physical action had been taken. Cole explained that he would be staying around with those he loved here until he could help put this right. He was accepting responsibility for what he had done and his love for his family was stronger than ever — he wanted to help them in whatever way he could.

I could sense that the communication was coming to a close. Cole's energy was starting to fade. His sister suddenly spoke out.

'Look at how she is sitting. Cole used to sit like that!'

I hadn't been aware of it until Cole's sister spoke but now I realised I was sitting rather awkwardly, in a very unusual position for someone wearing a skirt, with one leg up underneath me. It was how Cole always used to sit. That, together with the language I used, was additional evidence as far as Cole's sister was concerned, that Cole really was with them in the room and talking through me.

It was very clear that although there were many tears shed that afternoon, this time with their son and brother helped ease the family's pain of losing him from their physical lives.

Later we talked about the communication. It was then that I suddenly realised why the previous day's appointment had been 'missed'. It was to help the family release their anger. As a family they had loved Cole deeply and part of them was angry that he had taken his own life, but they weren't letting themselves feel that anger towards Cole because they loved him and they didn't like to get angry with him because they perceived they had just lost him out of their physical life. Their anger was being suppressed and it was stopping them all from moving through their grief.

Cole and his spirit world helpers knew this and that is where I came in. When I missed the appointment the day before, the family became angry with me — and rightly so. It is a lot easier to get angry with a complete stranger than with someone you have just lost. I was the vent for the anger. The release of the anger released a lot of energy and made the communication with Cole easier. It also helped the family to move through the grieving process.

And to think I had been scolding Spirit just the day before for not reminding me of the appointment. It was clearly another lesson for me to trust.

There have been many times at the shows and in private interviews with people when I have identified that it is suppressed anger keeping a person or family from moving through the grieving process. Interestingly, it isn't just those who take their own lives that we may need to feel angry towards. It can be anyone who leaves us.

In her book *On Death and Dying*, Elisabeth Kübler-Ross identifies five stages that people who have received catastrophic news go through:

1. Denial (This isn't happening to me!)
2. Anger (Why is this happening to me?)
3. Bargaining (I promise I'll be a better person if . . .)
4. Depression (I just don't care any more)
5. Acceptance (I am ready for whatever comes)

Kübler-Ross recognised that as people grieve, many seem to go through these five distinct stages of loss and experience a range of emotions. She also recognised that each person's grieving process is as unique for them as their own life is. Not everyone will go through all the emotions; some will spend longer in one stage than another, and the process certainly may not be linear, with some people moving forwards and backwards between the stages. Knowledge of the overall stages can be useful in terms of understanding how we move on after a bereavement but it shouldn't be seen as a defined process that we expect people to go through.

Many organisations today use a variation of Kübler-Ross's stages of grief to help their employees understand their reaction to loss and change.

Whenever you are faced with a change in life such as a redundancy or the end of a relationship, you will tend to go through these same stages. As you read through the different stages, try and relate them to either to your own past experiences or those of someone you know — this will help you get a real feel for the process so that you can recognise the different stages of it within yourself and within others in the future.

Denial

When a person dies, initially there is shock. Very quickly we then move into denial.

'This isn't happening to me.'

'It can't be true.'

'There must be some mistake.'

'I will wake up in a moment and all of this will have been a terrible dream.'

Denial behaviours may include still cooking extra food for our loved one, or expecting them to walk through the door any moment; in other words behaving as though they were still here. Some people describe this stage as disbelief.

Then we feel numb. Incapable of feeling our feelings. This emotional shutdown might get us through the funeral, but often we worry about what is wrong with us — why can't I feel? Why can't I cry?

As time passes and we allow ourselves to feel, we feel many different shades of fear. We fear that we won't see our loved one again. We fear that we won't be able to handle the feelings arising within us. We fear that we will not be able to cope without them in our lives — or with not seeing them again, not holding them again. Fear can be a terrifically powerful force.

The experience of fear is different for each of us. In extreme circumstances it can extend to fearing the loss of other loved ones, fearing for our own life and fearing having connections with others because we fear getting hurt again.

Then comes the anger.

Anger

Why is this happening to me? First we tend to get angry with someone else. Angry at the person who contributed to the death, the policeman, the doctor, the other driver. Angry at the article in the paper that didn't portray what happened fairly, angry at the judge for being too lenient. Angry at the doctor for not noticing the signs and running the tests. Angry at our loved one for not going to the doctor's. Angry at our loved one for leaving us or not saying goodbye. The list could go on and on. Somewhere along the line we find someone to blame and that is okay — it is part of the process to blame others and it helps us to feel our anger.

Then we blame ourselves. If only we had noticed the signs, taken the situation more seriously. If only we had spent more time with them, hopped on a plane as soon as we heard that they were ill. If only we hadn't said what we did to them all those years ago.

The torment goes on and on, and very often it can take us into depression.

Bargaining

This is where we may plead with God in whatever form we perceive God exists. 'I promise I will do whatever it takes if only you will make things as they were before.'

Depression

It is what it says, a depression of your energy. You have low energy and you feel lethargic; everything is an effort. You may not want to go out. You may find yourself crying uncontrollably, unable to stem the tears. You may feel that there is no light at the end of the tunnel. When you first experience depression it can hit you really hard and can be quite debilitating. You are stuck in a place you don't want to be, with feelings you don't want to feel. Very often depression is anger that has been suppressed.

This is where you perhaps doubt your ability to cope or move on. Take comfort in the fact that there is only one way to go and that is up, but not just yet. First you have to have understanding of the situation or at least your feelings about it.

Acceptance

With understanding comes acceptance and as you accept what is, the passing of your loved one and your feelings, you can move on. Your emotions — energy in motion — have passed through you and so you at last can move forward.

Even when you are moving on there can be days and even weeks or months that you find yourself pulled back into an earlier part of the process. Meeting someone who didn't know about your loved one's passing, seeing something that reminds you of them, reaching a significant date on the calendar. Somehow understanding that this is a process we all go through makes it easier.

So how do we help ourselves and others through this process? That is what we will be looking at in the next chapter.

R.I.P.

*I am the dew on fresh mown grass, the
    whispering of trees,
I am the morning sunrise and the gentle
    summer breeze.
I am the sound of silence, the moments you
    find peace,
I am much more than I once was and now
    I rest in peace.*

3. Helping Ourselves and Others to Grieve

Peter came to see me at the end of a show. He was a grey-haired gentleman in his mid-fifties. The lady by his side, who introduced him, was his sister. She did all the talking initially, and Peter looked a little uncomfortable even being there with her.

'My brother's wife died a couple of years ago,' Shirley explained.

Peter's eyes were misty and downcast. I could really feel his discomfort at being put in this situation.

'We were all hoping that his wife would come through tonight but she hasn't.'

Peter looked up hopefully. I could see that the

loss of his wife was almost too much to bear and that, as uncomfortable as it was asking for help, it was better than the pain of not knowing.

'I am really tired,' I said apologetically. 'I may not be able to do anything for you, but if you wait till the end I will see what I can do.'

The family took seats and I continued working my way through the queue of people, answering questions and signing their books. It was a long queue and each person in their own way needed my assistance. Some took longer than others.

Before I had finished signing books, Anne, Peter's wife in spirit world, was with me. I hurriedly finished seeing the last few people and then quietened myself, ready to listen to her. The family gathered around hopefully.

'Today would have been your wedding anniversary!' I exclaimed.

Immediately I knew I had their full attention. They had arranged to come to the show on the anniversary. I was amazed. Clearly this was one message that I really needed to convey tonight. I wondered why didn't she come through at the show. The reply came back straight away. 'Too emotional.' Anne was a private person, as Peter was, and what she had to say was not for all to hear. Peter nodded; he understood exactly what she meant.

For the next twenty minutes or so Anne talked through me. They had six children together. She had been riddled with cancer. Peter had nursed her at home throughout and he never moaned once. She had always felt it should be her nursing him, not the other way around. He had been so patient with her, so very kind, tending to her every need. Theirs was a very special love. They had been sweethearts at thirteen and rarely had so much as a cross word. Peter had been inconsolable in his grief. He had lost his wife, the mother of his children and his best friend all at once. How could he go on? Should he go on?

That was why I had needed to see him in private after the show and that was why the show was on the anniversary of their marriage. His pain was peaking as he remembered their time together and how much he missed her. It physically hurt him.

'When will I stop grieving?' he pleaded. 'Sometimes I just don't think I can go on, but I have to because of the kids.' Peter's sister reached over to touch his arm, to somehow share his pain. Peter was hurting with the loss of his wife, and Peter's sister was hurting seeing him in so much pain. He had been moving on with his grief but the wedding anniversary had brought all the pain back once more. He despaired of putting such grief behind him.

The room was very quiet. My words when they came were barely audible.

'I think it is the pain of loss that you really want to avoid, not the grief.'

Peter was still looking down, feeling his pain.

'Grief is the healing process that helps us deal with the loss of a loved one,' I gently explained. 'The pain you are feeling is the pain of loss.'

I knew I had to be extremely gentle with him. It was a few moments before I spoke again. 'When you love another person you connect to them energetically. When they move from this physical dimension there can be a physical pain.'

'That's what I feel,' he said, 'that's it. I physically hurt.' He looked up at me for the first time in several minutes. I could feel his physical pain and I knew that sometimes it felt like it was too much pain to bear.

'Grief is the internal reflection of that physical loss. As you allow yourself to grieve you allow yourself to heal the pain.'

I could see that in some small way my words were making a difference.

'We may never get over the loss of someone but we do learn to live with that loss. It does become more bearable. They say that time is the greatest healer and it is true. There will come a time that you will remember her and honour her without feeling the pain that you do now. You get to that place by allowing yourself to grieve, by allowing yourself to feel the feelings and by feeling your love for her. Your love for her is vast.'

I smiled at him. 'It is harder at the moment because it is your anniversary. Birthdays, Christmas and anniversaries always bring our unresolved feelings to the fore.'

Peter nodded, his eyes brimming with tears.

'Grieve for as long as you need to — grieve until you heal.'

I have come to recognise that our society places enormous pressure on us to get over loss, to get through the grief and on with our lives. But how long do you grieve for a wife of forty years? A son killed on a motorbike? A four-year-old daughter who drowned? A year? Five years? Forever? The loss happens in an instant, but we experience the repercussions throughout the rest of our lives. Losses such as these change us. They change who we are.

This next story is another that happened after a show. 'Nana' had wanted to bring Katy, her granddaughter of seven, to the show as she had recently lost her dad but Mum, Nana's daughter, didn't think it was a good idea. Nana had come to see me at the end of the show to see if there was anything that I could say to either Mum or Katy, neither of whom were present.

Generally speaking my show is not really the place for children, as the emotions can be too intense. There are other ways we can support children through their grief.

On the rare occasions that a child has come to a show and I have been guided to pass on a message, this has always been done in private with the parent or guardian present.

As I was explaining all this to Nana I started to feel a male presence with me — Martin. It was he who had wanted his daughter there, not Nana. Nana had just been picking up on what he wanted. Nana, his mother-in-law, was in less emotional turmoil than his wife was and he had hoped that as her mother, she would be able to influence his wife to let Katy come to the show. Nana agreed she had thought it was what Martin wanted, but never told her daughter this as she was afraid it might upset her to know that she could sense Martin and yet her daughter couldn't.

Unfortunately, the opportunity to attend the show had passed now. We were travelling on to the next town early the following day, so there would be no time for me to see Katy or her mum.

'What else can I do to help?' I asked internally.

Martin indicated that Katy needed to spend more time with Nana. Mum needed time to grieve and Katy did too. Mum had too much on her plate trying to be a single parent for the first time and coping with her own loss. Katy wouldn't talk about it. Mum had tried. It was different for Katy. In pictures he showed me that Katy needed to talk with other kids who had experienced a loss, so that she didn't feel so alone.

Martin could see that Katy and Mum would both stay stuck without this — each was trying to be strong for the other. He loved them both so much.

Nana understood exactly what he meant. She had wondered about some kind of bereavement counselling for Mum, but she hadn't realised that it might be available for Katy too.

'Thank you,' she said. 'I know what to do now.' Martin had simply confirmed her own feelings about the situation.

This story and many others like it remind us of the value of bereavement support groups.

Support groups provide you with a safe place to talk about your loss with others who are experiencing similar feelings. Local bereavement groups are usually facilitated by your local hospital, hospice, counselling center and/or place of worship.

Helping someone to make that first appointment for bereavement counselling can be a really positive step to take and there are other things you can do for yourself or someone else depending on their stage in the bereavement process. Remember always that this bereavement process is not set in stone, it is merely a guide, and bereavement affects each of us very differently. Remember also that children need support with the bereavement process as well.

So how can we support each other through the different stages of grieving?

The initial stage of shock, denial and numbness is really nature's way of helping us to survive the loss. Shock immobilises us — sometimes literally — and we cease to function. Sweet tea is an age-old remedy for shock. Sitting with a person can also help.

Denial ensures that the feelings are paced in such a way that we can handle them.

It is okay to ask 'How can I help?' but do bear in mind that you may not get much of a response because at this stage in the process people are so lost in their own sorrow that they are not likely to be thinking very clearly. It is perhaps better just to do the things you see need doing: taking out the rubbish, bringing in a cooked meal or running an errand for them.

During denial, our focus is on the past. We feel the loss of a situation that we were comfortable with and confident about. We want things to 'get back to normal'. This stage is all about being gentle with ourselves and simply getting through each day. Numbness is our way of saying, 'I really don't want to deal with this.'

As we move forward into anger, the second stage of grieving, we may find ourselves responding by finding someone to blame. By focusing our emotions on a particular person or organisation, blame allows us to temporarily avoid facing up to our feelings about the death of our loved one. Blaming someone else is easier than allowing ourselves to experience the pain of loss, and it pushes out of our minds any fears and anxieties we have about the changes that our loved one's passing will cause.

After blaming someone else, often we then fall into blaming ourselves: 'if only I had done X or not done Y.' You can help someone through this stage by helping them put the situation into perspective.

Jean was a lovely lady who was finding it very hard to come to terms with her son's sudden death. Jeremy was in his early thirties when he died. It had been a freak accident, a fall downstairs, that had led to his death. Jeremy had been a perpetual student and had been reluctant to fly the nest, but, encouraged by family, Jean had helped him financially into his own home just six months before he died. Mum felt that had she not 'pushed him out of his home' he would still be alive. She was angry with herself and was clearly blaming herself for her son's death.

Jeremy came through from spirit world to say that he was fine. It had simply been his time. He had done all he wanted to here; he had been ready to go. 'You didn't push me out,' he said. 'You gave me a helping hand to stand on my own two feet when I needed it. If I had died on the stairs at your home would you be sitting here wishing you had given me that helping hand to set up in my own place?'

Jean nodded. She couldn't bring herself to speak for a few moments but we both recognised the truth in his words. Where he was living was not important. He had been ready to pass on from this physical place and start learning about the spiritual side of life. Mum laughed. That was her Jeremy — a perpetual learner.

Our minds can do dreadful things to us when we lose a loved one.

We can feel guilty for all we did or didn't do. Sometimes there's a grain of truth in what we think; other times it is just nonsense, designed to take our attention out of this present moment and what we are feeling right now and into the mind. The mind likes to have our attention all of the time, and will stop at nothing to do this. And yet it is a time that we should perhaps be in our feelings, feeling the pain of loss and the depth of our love for those we have lost.

The more we can consciously take ourselves out of the mind and its ramblings and into what we are feeling right now, the better.

This is often a good time to start bereavement counselling as we may find it hard to express our feelings at this stage. How do you put into words the pain of losing someone who has been a part of your life for so long, or for whom you have such deep feelings?

We may fear sounding foolish to those around us as we try to help them understand just what we are going through, or we may fear showing them just how vulnerable we really are. Bereavement counselling can not only help us feel and express our anger towards our loved one for dying and towards God/life for taking them, but can also help us access other emotions, including the pain of loss. Each stage of the grieving process takes as long as it needs to. Writing about our feelings and talking to others can help. As we talk, be it in our own heads or to another, we gradually start to let go of the past and start thinking about how we will adapt to the new situation. As we start thinking about how we are going to cope in the future, we may then experience a period of self-doubt.

If we don't allow ourselves access to our feelings then it is likely depression will follow. Depression occurs when our energy is literally depressed. When we hold our feelings in, they get stuck inside us, and we get stuck in our physical lives too. Getting out of bed in the morning may be difficult and we may not care about how we look or what we eat. There is no interest in life or in hobbies or other things that used to interest us.

One of the things that really stands out for me with people who are depressed is how they always look down, almost to the floor, their heads bent over — and it seems that they are looking for answers in that place. When I studied Neuro-Linguistic Programming (NLP) I learned that where we hold our eyes can be an indicator of what is going on within a person.

Take a few moments to try out these simple exercises for yourself.

Ask yourself to visualise your toothbrush and see what colour it is. Notice what happens with your eyes. Where do they move to access this information?

Now visualise your front door and see in your mind's eye what is immediately to the right of your door. Again notice what happens with your eyes. Where do they move to 'find' this information?

Now picture an elephant in a pink tutu dancing a pirouette. What happened with your eyes that time?

About 85 per cent of the population find visual memories up and to the left. We find created or imagined images up and to the right. For the other 15 per cent of the population the information is stored in different places, so just notice where it is stored for you.

Now, think about someone you love dearly. Where did your eyes go? Most people, again about 85 per cent, will find that their eyes go down and to the right as they think about this because they are accessing feelings.

Let's try an interesting little experiment.

Look up and talk to yourself in that critical/ negative way you sometimes do. (You knew you shouldn't have done that, didn't you; don't you ever learn; and so on.)

Keep your eyes up. Don't you just want to laugh at that silly voice? I know I do. The voice that can sometimes really get me down sounds so silly when my eyes are looking up — I can't take it seriously.

Now let's try eyes down and to the right and try making yourself feel enthusiastic. Tell yourself how wonderful you are, how perfect your life is. All that positive self talk just doesn't touch you, does it?

Isn't that amazing? So how could it help here? Remember the old saying, 'chin up'? Perhaps in doing that literally we lift our gaze, broaden our perspective and start to change our view on life. Getting a person who is very down to look up — at nature, at you, at the birds in the sky — may help, even if only momentarily. The only way to know for sure is to try it for yourself. See how it affects you.

Diet and exercise are key allies for getting through depression. Some foods lower our energy; sugar and carbohydrates may give us a quick fix but then after the high comes the low. Eating good-quality fruit and vegetables (organic when you can get them) helps, then your body isn't battling against pesticides and other chemicals. Invest in a juicer — if your body doesn't have to use energy chewing and breaking down the food there is more energy left for you. Moderate exercise such as walking, cycling and swimming gets energy moving through us and gets the emotions moving through us too. As you exercise you literally work through the issues that you are holding. Fresh air is also good for us, as are sunshine, feeding ducks, walking along the beach and generally doing anything that you would usually enjoy.

Being around young children can also do us a power of good — watch them, see how fully present they are in this moment, feel how alive they feel.

Anything can take us out of our present feelings, if we let it. Our minds can only hold one thought at a time and if we replace the painful thought with a less painful thought, the feeling running through us will change and our energy levels will also be affected.

It can be very difficult allowing someone we love to go through this stage. We want them to be back like they used to be and their behaviour may make us feel powerless. But there are some practical things that can and do help.

Take someone to the park, to a movie, out for dinner — anything that will help them get out of their selves. A little and often seems to work best. We give them the time they need and we help them to see things differently every now and then, or give them something else to focus on.

As the feelings are gradually processed we may then move to the final stage in the grieving process: understanding, acceptance and moving on.

I personally think that this is the best stage for someone to see a medium. Prior to this there can be too much pain, too many heavy emotions in their energy field. How long it is after the loved one's passing varies enormously, and remember these stages are not set in stone: elements of all five stages may be present in one day. The fastest I have ever known spirit-world communication was twenty-four hours after passing, but this was a lady who had worked as a medium herself and communication was very brief. On average it is at least six months to get a meaningful communication, but in practice there have been many good examples of communi-cation after just two or three months. I allow myself to be guided by Spirit on this.

As we move through the acceptance stage we can still feel the pain of loss but we are looking to understand what has happened and perhaps looking for a higher meaning of life for ourselves and our loved one. Death in and of itself doesn't make sense. What is the point if we just die? What is the point of any of it?

We also start exploring how we might cope without our loved one. One of the things I have learned over the years about the pain of loss and the grieving process is that our love really does hold all the pain. It would not hurt so much if we did not love them so much. By focusing on the love we feel, which is still so real, we become more aware of our loved one on a non-physical level. We always were connected with them but now it becomes our primary connection with them and this link can never be taken away. This non-physical connection or soul connection awareness also serves us well when it is our time to pass away.

By keeping our awareness in our hearts rather than our heads throughout the bereavement process we can focus on the love that connects rather than the pain of separation. We can move more quickly into peace, when we are ready.

The mind runs through thought after thought to get our attention constantly. Could the passing of a loved one pain us so greatly that we would have to keep our awareness in our hearts just to stay sane? And if we did that for long enough, would that be sufficient to take us into enlightenment? I believe so.

If part of the soul's learning here is the opening of our heart's centre, what better than the illusion of losing someone we love to truly help us to feel?

And why would the soul wish to open the physical heart? Without us experiencing the pain of loss and feeling for one another, how could we ever hope to feel true compassion towards our fellow human beings? Compassion is the sincere desire to relieve another from their pain and suffering. Without compassion in our hearts would we ever have any chance of living in a peaceful world?

Viewed from a spiritual perspective, death certainly seems to make more sense than when viewed through purely physical eyes. If this spiritual perspective makes the pain of loss less painful to bear then perhaps it is a useful one for us to consider further.

IF I WERE STILL ALIVE...

If I were still alive
My heart would beat for you,
I'd want to hold you in my arms and tell
you what I knew.
I'd find a way of telling you that really
I'm all right,
I'd find a way of kissing you before
you slept at night,
I'd use your dreams to contact you and
show you that I care,
I'd whisper to you in the night and gently
stroke your hair.
I'd love you when you're lonely and
embrace you when you're down.
I'd kiss away your heartfelt tears and wipe
away your frown.
I'd do all this not knowing if you would
ever see,
My love is all around you and ever more
will be.

4. Murders and Missing People

'Could you look at this for me?' A red-haired lady was holding a faded photo of a child for me to see. I had to really focus to make out the details in the dim light of the theatre foyer. I was feeling very content.

When you do a truly beautiful show, you may be physically tired but you feel amazing because you know that everyone in the audience has been touched by the experience. I was about halfway through the queue of waiting people. Some wanted books signed; others wanted to give me a hug or ask me a question.

I had just finished signing the book in front of me when, unthinkingly, I found myself taking the photo in both hands. It looked quite old, not black and white but then not colour either. I guessed it had been colour once but had faded with time. In it was the image of a young girl, a pretty wee thing, probably about eight or nine, not much more. I found myself pointing at the lady who had presented the photograph.

'You weren't there,' I said quite abruptly. She nodded silently, confirming she wasn't around at the time of the young girl's passing.

'A wavy line' and 'way' came out of my mouth, and the rest of me was wondering what this was all about. The girl in the photo was in my body and in my head now. She was showing me that she had been stabbed and walked part of the *way* herself. Her footsteps faltered, taking her in a *wavy line*, as she was losing so much blood. She didn't know where to go for help. I could really feel her distress now.

'She didn't know where to go for help,' I said anxiously.

Then, just as suddenly as she had spoken through me, I felt how she felt as her spirit lifted out of her physical body. She was showing me the whole area cordoned off below her floating spirit.

'It's cordoned off. There are blue lights — policemen are combing the area,' I explained.

'After she "died" her spirit self rose up out of her physical body and she watched as the whole area was cordoned off and the policemen combed the area, looking for clues. She was murdered.' I could see everything she had seen.

'I didn't feel any pain,' she reassured through me after a moment or two.

'I didn't feel any fear. I just felt . . .' I could feel her searching within me for the right word.

'I just felt . . . distress.' I understood what she meant. She was confused, disorientated. She didn't know what was happening to her. She didn't know where to go for help — that had been worrying her more than her injury.

'Then I felt peace, profound peace,' the young girl explained through me and as she did so, I too was filled with the most exquisite and indescribable peace.

Further images and sensations followed, too numerous to describe.

'She is showing me that was then, and this is now. Now she is safe. You need to know that,' I said, finding myself looking at a gentleman whose eyes I could just catch over the shoulder of the lady. The red-haired lady standing in front of me was crying. She explained that the girl's death happened twenty-seven years ago.

'She is safe. No one, nothing can hurt or harm her now — she is safe,' I reassured them both.

It was then that I found myself looking out into a sea of intrigued faces. I was suddenly very aware of the present and I realised I had a crowd of onlookers — people still waiting to have their books signed. I hadn't intended the young girl's spirit to come through while I was signing books — it just happened as I looked at the photo.

'I will need to see you privately,' I quickly explained to the lady and gentleman in front of me, directing them over to a seated area where they would be able to wait.

They waited patiently as I finished signing books. I was keeping the young girl in my space but not allowing her to overpower me again. I could see that many of the onlookers would have loved to have stayed too, but it really wasn't appropriate. This one needed to be done in private.

It was a little while before I could let Jessica, the girl in the photo, back into me fully. When I did she wanted to talk to Dad. Dad was the man whose eyes I had connected with just moments before. She knew her father, even though it had been twenty-seven years. Their love was what connected them and always would. She loved her dad.

In private Jessica had a lot more to tell. What Dad needed now was understanding. He needed to understand why his daughter had died and perhaps more importantly why she had died in the terrible way that she had. In my head I was concerned. How could this one ever be explained or understood?

Jessica showed me a past life of her father's. In that previous incarnation he had been a very religious man, a priest, and had devoted himself to his spiritual practice. In this incarnation he had chosen to develop forgiveness, of himself and others. Jessica explained to me that he was 90 per cent through his ordeal, but the images of what had happened or might have happened to his beautiful, innocent daughter remained in his head.

All that Jessica told me I conveyed, and the red-haired lady confirmed that Jessica had been sexually violated before she was killed. The details were sketchy but there definitely had been some kind of sexual abuse. To this day, Dad couldn't even speak of it.

Jessica wasn't going into the particulars — that wouldn't help. Jessica wanted to wipe the slate clean for Dad: to take away the thoughts, the images and the feelings. She hadn't known what was happening to her. She knew she was hurt but the biggest anxiety for her had been not knowing where to go for help. She had been such a good girl and always wanted to do the right thing. It had worried her that she was not doing the right thing when she didn't know where to go for help. That had been her main concern — not the images in Dad's head that were torturing him. She wanted him to let those images go.

More than anything Jessica wanted Dad to know that now she was at peace. Completely at peace. What had happened to her wasn't important; what was important was how she was now. She was at peace and she wanted to help Dad be at peace. She wanted to share her peace and help Dad move through forgiveness into peace.

'Tell him I can't get through to him when he is in his mind so much. He needs to stop thinking about it all and replaying it all in his head. He won't find peace in his head.' I knew what Jessica was trying to convey — worrying won't take you into peace; it never does, it just keeps you in worry. The mind tries to make you think that if you reflect on a subject just a little more you will work it all out, but you don't. You just end up staying in the mind and worrying more.

Dad had got better about 'switching off' but every now and then when he was tired or run down it would all come in on him again and it would take him days to come right. He used not to be like this.

'Tell him not to think,' said Jessica. 'It's the thinking that is causing the pain.'

I knew what she meant but wasn't so sure that Dad would understand. In my head I asked her: 'What should he do instead?'

'Just relax and feel me, feel that I am around. Communicate with me in feelings rather than words. Words confuse things. Feelings are clearer to perceive. He can show me how he is feeling and I can show him how at peace I am now. The peace and love will always overpower the pain, if he lets himself feel me.' There was a pause while I conveyed to Dad what Jessica had said and then she continued.

'The pain is his creation. It is based on his mental perception of what happened and how I suffered, but it's not real: none of it is. I am here and I am at peace. But he has no way of knowing this until he steps out of his mind and into his open heart. Tell him that is where he will find me — in his heart.'

I understood exactly what Jessica meant, for my heart is where I find the spirit-world loved-ones at my shows. I didn't know exactly how ready Dad was to take all of this in. I did my best and Jessica seemed pleased with how far we got that night. I felt her spirit withdraw and move across to Dad. How I wished he could perceive her in the way that I could. Surely that would take away some of his pain and shatter the illusion of Jessica's death.

It was getting late and the communication with Jessica had come to a close. I knew that in time as Dad learned to spend less time in his head, thinking about what may or may not have happened, he would find himself letting go of all the thoughts and pictures and feelings that he associated with Jessica's passing. It was these images and resultant feelings that were causing him so much pain. Over time, the more he let the images of the past go, the more he would be fully present, and the more fully present he was the more likely it would be that he could sense his beautiful daughter's presence and love.

It was clear it wasn't going to happen overnight. There were still a lot of feelings for Dad to work through and process, but at least the seeds had been sown and Jessica was with him. I was so pleased that Jessica had been able to come through as clearly as she had. It must have given Dad and his partner a lot of comfort, and it certainly was a communication that needed to be done in private.

It was only a couple of shows later that I was asked about what happens to the soul of someone who had been murdered. The question took me by surprise. I have been asked many times what happens to the soul of someone who takes their own life but this was the first time someone had asked me about the soul of someone who had been murdered. Part of me was surprised that the question should even be asked but then I sometimes forget that not everybody has had the experiences I have.

In both cases the soul goes through to wherever it is ready to go, based on the soul's ability to feel and express love. If the soul is open and loving it will go into a loving dimension and if it resonates from a place of fear it will go through to a more fearful dimension.

There is no hell, although some of the more fear-based realms may appear quite unpleasant to a loving person. To a fearful person the place feels the same as they do inside and so it is not a 'hell' — instead it feels comfortable to them.

As I was explaining this to the audience I found myself sensing the presence of the gentleman concerned. I knew that he was keen to communicate with me but recognised that because his had been quite a recent passing and a very violent one this would best be handled backstage.

I quickly finished my very brief response to the question, explaining that our souls cannot ever be harmed, and reassuring the family that Arthur was safely through into the spiritual dimensions. Arthur wanted to talk to them there and then but because of the violent nature of his passing I knew it would be best to see them in private after the show. They readily agreed and so it was a couple of hours before I could continue the message.

As soon as I could I went over to the waiting area where the family was seated and then instead of sitting down as I was intending to do, I found myself walking around the chair in quite a casual manner. I observed myself and what was happening within me.

'This gentleman was strolling, just strolling,' I said, describing how 'ordinary' it all felt. I turned to the group of three ladies who had been waiting so patiently.

'This must be to do with how he died,' I said. 'He is showing me that he was just walking.'

'He was,' came the quick response.

I continued to stroll. I felt a man, younger than me, come at me. There was a struggle, pain. It all happened quickly. I conveyed what I was experiencing as fully as I could.

'He was attacked. It was completely out of the blue by someone he didn't know. He is bewildered. What is going on? What is happening? There are people all around, but they are people he doesn't know.'

Flashes of what Arthur could see were going through my head. He wasn't alone. There were people around him. He hadn't known his attacker. The attack had been completely unprovoked. He told me he wasn't a bad man. It was a waste of a good life.

'I can see people standing around. I have been hit with something — I can feel it — long and thin.' All eyes looked down, including my own, to my hands — which were at about waist height — holding something. I couldn't see it but I could feel it. I was losing a lot of blood.

'He was stabbed,' the family explained.

I crouched, holding my stomach — I knew he had died of blood loss and said this. If he had been stabbed just an inch either way he would probably have lived. It was exactly right. Arthur's sister explained that the wound had severed an artery.

Arthur had not been in spirit world long. It had been a hell of a shock to him, going like that. He had picked a few fights in his time and I think the family would have understood if one of those had led to his death but this attack appeared entirely unprovoked.

In spirit world Arthur had two guardians with him who looked a lot like monks.

As far as I could tell they were helping Arthur control his mental and emotional reactions to the murder in a way that would not cause him further harm. It was only the second time I had seen anything like that.

Arthur did have quite a temper on him and he would have been a hard man to live with. He wasn't taking his death at someone else's hands that well. He still couldn't see why he had died — why him?

Arthur had just been in the wrong place at the wrong time. A man with severe mental health issues had been on the rampage. He had killed someone else in a neighbouring building before heading out onto the street and straight into Arthur's path.

I talked with Arthur's family for quite a while. They were happy he was okay. I think the talk of the two monks with him mystified them but everything else had made perfect sense. They could be at peace knowing he was okay.

I have worked with several families whose loved ones have been murdered or died in suspicious circumstances. It is demanding work. The worst times are when a person is missing, presumed dead, and the family are hoping that you will help them find them alive. Then, as the days pass, they just hope you will help them to find a body.

I can count on one hand the number of people whose bodies I have helped to search for. It is *really* unpleasant work. The families are distraught, tired and weary from the pain of not knowing. They have painstakingly gone over the movements of their loved ones again and again, with police and in their own time. They have gone through their loved ones' diaries, emails, text messages, phone books looking for any clue, however small. Believe me, it is nothing at all like you see on your television screens.

Lives stop. The pain goes on. The families have tried to work it out logically and intuitively and drawn a blank and that is where I have been brought in. Always by the families, never by the police. I work with those the deceased has a loving connection with and the purpose is to bring resolution and closure, not entertainment for our television screens.

The families often find me through a previous family who have had my help and this was the case with Simon's family.

Simon's father came to see me a few weeks after his disappearance. The police were treating his disappearance as a missing person case, not a murder investigation, as Dad's car had been broken into and one of the documents taken was Simon's passport.

Often when a body is missing, the spirit of the person is not at rest as they know their family are looking for them. I couldn't find Simon on the spiritual dimensions but I did find Bert and Gladys, Dad's grandparents. They confirmed that Simon had died and his spirit was with his younger brother, who was still alive and out looking for the body.

Dad confirmed that the brother was looking for Simon's body as we spoke. The grandparents gave me a visual description of where the body was, and when the police eventually searched in this area Simon's body was found within 300 metres of where I had described.

Simon's spirit moved over and found peace once he had seen that the body had been found. It is not always this easy. If a person is murdered, or if their body is not found, the spirit is rarely at peace initially. Instead of moving straight through into spirit world as would normally happen, the spirit stays earthbound on a dimension commonly termed the astral plane.

This means that as a medium I cannot find them in the usual spiritual dimensions. Instead, I have to go onto the astral plane to locate them. In spirit world the energy is loving and light, compared to here. This is not the case with the astral plane. There is an added complication — I get to feel everything the deceased felt and feel it with a vividness that sometimes makes me forget who I am. It can be scary work and is not for the faint-hearted. To even 'survive' on this plane you have to learn not to fear anything and you have to have absolute control of your thoughts. Your thoughts become your reality very quickly in this dimension and thinking a fearful thought can very quickly take you into a very frightened state. Start feeling fear, and other fearful beings will be drawn into your space. This is a place where it can be all too easy to lose your sanity, so I avoid it wherever I can.

My partner Andrew is more geared up to doing this kind of work than I am, but on occasions I have had to do my own dirty work. Thankfully Andrew has been able to coach and guide me through the more difficult times and has helped me get out of trouble when I have bitten off more than I can chew. When Andrew bites off more than he can chew — well, then it gets really interesting! And neither of us might sleep for a few nights!

It can take me an arduous couple of weeks to help a spirit on the astral plane pass over to the right place in spirit world. There is a horrendous catch-22 situation: they do not want to pass over till their body is found and I cannot communicate with them properly until they pass over into the appropriate spiritual dimension.

It's an impasse that can last for days — and all the time I feel how they felt, not able to properly function in physical life. My kids have literally lost Mum for a couple of weeks at a time when I have been working on such cases and it is because of this that I now decline such work. There are other mediums who are better suited to it. It has been a hard decision for me to make but this work really does push the bounds of my sanity — something I am not prepared to gamble with, for my family's sake as well as my own.

It has been through this kind of work that I have really questioned what I do and why I do it. Thankfully there are many other times that spirit communication is beautiful and inspiring — and it is because of these moments that I *know* beyond a shadow of a doubt that I am exactly where I am supposed to be, doing exactly what I am supposed to be doing.

5. Spirits That Don't Rest

I could see that the lady in front of me had been crying. Her eyes were still red from all the emotion and lines where the tears had been flowing still streaked her face.

'I need some help,' she blurted. 'It's my son Brett; he is seeing his daddy in the wardrobe at night and it is really frightening him. I don't know what to do.' She was sobbing uncontrollably now and I had to get the lady assisting me with the books to sit with her for a while.

When I was able to sit with her I found she was feeling a little better. One of the questions asked during the show had made her realise that the images her little boy was seeing were likely to be real. Jennifer's partner Rob had taken his own life just a few months before and just about every other night since her youngest child Brett, who was only four, had been terrified of sleeping in his own bed. He kept claiming he was seeing Daddy in the wardrobe and on the end of his bed.

'At first I just thought it was his way of getting into my bed to sleep,' she explained. 'It has been really hard for all of us. I thought it was his way of getting a few extra cuddles from me. I expected it to pass and just be a phase but it hasn't — it's getting worse. It is nearly every night now and he seems genuinely afraid when he comes running to me. He is getting so that he doesn't want to go to bed at night because he's afraid of seeing Daddy.' I could really feel her distress.

'I just don't know what to do, what to tell him. Is it possible that he really is seeing Rob?' she asked.

Internally I asked for guidance. I couldn't find Rob on the spiritual dimensions that I usually access at the shows and that made it more likely that he was earthbound and on the astral plane.

'Tell me more about what Brett experiences,' I prompted.

'He goes to sleep and I look in on him before I go to bed. He seems really peaceful and then at 2 am or maybe 3 am he's crying and screaming. He says he has seen Daddy in the wardrobe.'

'Has he got out of bed and gone to the wardrobe?' I asked, needing more clarification.

'No, he's still in bed — the wardrobe door is still closed so I think he means he's having nightmares and seeing Daddy in the wardrobe. When he wakes up we have to go and look in the wardrobe to make sure Daddy is not there. He's usually so shook up I just take him into my bed with me; it's the only way I can get him to settle.'

It sounded to me that Brett's dream of seeing Daddy in the wardrobe could be symbolic of Daddy being trapped on the astral plane. I needed to check this theory out.

'Does he ever see Daddy while he is awake?' I asked.

'Sometimes.'

I nodded for Jennifer to go on.

'It's not nearly so frequent as the nightmares but there have probably been half a dozen times when he has come running in to tell me Daddy is sitting on the end of his bed and that Daddy won't stop crying.'

Spirits that are earthbound often have more negative emotion with them than spirits in spirit world, and Brett's description of his father crying on the end of his bed made sense to me. It seemed more than likely that Brett really was seeing his Dad but I still had to ask some more questions to fully understand what was happening. Seeing Daddy while he was awake meant that Brett was perhaps able to perceive the astral plane while conscious.

'Has Brett ever talked about seeing anyone else? Invisible friends or anything like that?' I asked.

'No.'

'Just Dad?'

'Yes.'

'I am sorry to have so many questions for you, but I need to know what is happening. Did Brett see your husband cry a lot before his passing?' I asked. I was curious to see if he was just projecting his memories of Daddy to help him process his own feelings.

'No, Rob kept all his problems to himself. We tried talking but I only seemed to help him go around in circles, or he would end up getting mad with me. I don't think Brett ever saw his daddy cry.'

'Just one more question,' I said. 'Did Daddy's moods ever frighten Brett?' I gently asked.

'No, he really did try and keep out of our way when he was down — he just locked himself in the basement. I feel so awful really. I should have helped him more than I did.'

We talked a little longer and it became increasingly clear that this was not just a case of Brett remembering having Daddy around. Brett hadn't seen him cry like that and he certainly was never scared of Daddy as he was now. More likely than not Rob was still earthbound as a spirit and Brett, as well as seeing him, was sensing his grief — and this level of adult emotion was frightening him. It was more than he could cope with.

With cases such as this the work can be done with the family member affected or directly with the loved one who has passed over. Clearly Brett was very young and had already seen and experienced enough, so it would be a case of communicating with Dad and talking to him about the distress his behaviour was causing, persuading him to move on and let go of all the thoughts and feelings that were keeping him earthbound.

Andrew is much more experienced than I am at helping souls across. He does it during the shows when asked either by people here or by souls that are wanting to move on. Helping Rob was something we would be able to sort out later that night. Now my main concern was Jennifer.

'And how are you getting on?' I gently asked.

'Okay.'

It was an okay that screamed 'I'm not!'

'Really?' I asked, concerned about how she was handling it all.

'No,' Jennifer blurted. The tears were flowing freely again.

Our 'natural' reaction when someone cries like this is often to put our arm around them, but I have learned not to do this. Often we put our arms around the other person to stop the person from crying, because it feels uncomfortable for us. I have learned to accept my discomfort and to allow people to cry for as long at they need, then, when the tears have finished, I give them a hug. Sometimes it can take a while, but crying is good for us: it heals the pain of loss.

It took a little while but eventually Jennifer was ready to talk again.

'I know he's in a better place. I just wish I could have helped.' I understood what she meant. Rob had been busy giving me information while Jennifer wept.

'You do know that he was mentally ill, that this wasn't just a depression?' I asked when the timing felt right.

Jennifer nodded. She had known that his behaviour was really not 'right'. He had been hurting himself, inflicting wounds on his body, burning his own flesh.

'He wouldn't let me get help,' she cried.

It was true — he would have killed her and the children first. We both knew this and somehow I think it helped having me understand the position she was in. No one else had understood until now. His mother had blamed Jennifer for the problems in the marriage and thus the situation had been particularly difficult for Jennifer to bear sometimes. She knew that in a way Rob's passing had been a release. For all of them, not just Rob.

'This was his only way out . . . the only one he could see. He didn't want to lose you and the kids. He was afraid his children would be taken from him,' I explained, based on what Rob had told me.

'I know, I know,' she nodded. Jennifer knew that she couldn't really have looked after him and the kids. The kids were not safe around him at times.

'I just wish I could have done something to help. I wish I could have found a way, somehow.'

For a time Jennifer and I looked at each other. For Rob there simply hadn't been another way. I had the feeling that no matter what she had tried it would always have ended this way because of how he was inside. His passing was in many ways a blessing. Now at last he had a chance of being at peace.

I knew I had to be really firm with Jennifer to help her get through what she was feeling.

Part of her, as much as she loved Rob, was glad that the ordeal they shared was over — and she felt guilty about that. It was her guilt that was halting the grieving process.

Every day she could see how much her children were missing Daddy and every day she was feeling that she could have done more. If only she had been more patient, if only she could have found him the right kind of help. If only she had listened more, been more tolerant.

The guilt was misplaced. Rob told me very firmly that his passing was his choice not hers, that there was nothing she could have done to keep him here once he had made the decision to leave. I conveyed what he said as firmly as he had spoken to me.

'Look. You did everything you could. You really did. This was his choice, not yours. For your children's sake you have to stop doing this to yourself and accept that it was his choice. He has made it and now it's about you and the kids moving on from here.

'I will do what I can to help him move over. Your job is to concentrate on the kids and you.'

Jennifer nodded. I felt as though Rob really had got through to her at last that this was his choosing, not hers. All of it, even the mental health condition, had been his choosing at some level. Her choice was to be with the kids and help them move on as best she could, and she had all the abilities she needed to do this.

We talked more and I was able to reassure Jennifer that Rob's spirit would not be so troublesome to Brett from now on. Later that evening, Andrew would ensure he moved through to the right place for him. Rob's spirit was already feeling much more peaceful, having got off his chest all that he needed to say. The family moving on would help him feel less bad about all the pain he had caused them.

I gave Jennifer my phone number and asked her to call me the following day to see if Brett had had a better night. When we arrived home Andrew worked with Rob to help him lift his vibration and move through into the appropriate dimension.

A whole week passed before I heard from Jennifer. It turned out to be a good sign. Brett was still reluctant to go to bed because he remembered the frightening dreams but at least the screaming in the night had stopped and he was managing to spend the whole night in his own bed. Jennifer was very grateful and we agreed that she would call me in another week to let me know if all was still going well. Two weeks passed and I thought we might have successfully sorted the situation, but no, the nightmares had returned once more, not as bad this time but he had been up twice that week. Jennifer wanted to know what was happening.

Later that evening Andrew and I took a look. This time we had no trouble finding Rob in the spirit world dimensions he had passed into successfully. He still wasn't very happy; he felt he had messed a lot of things up and was still mad with himself, but this was better than the depressed state he had been in before. He had tried to come through to let the family know he was okay. His son had a birthday coming up. He hadn't meant to scare Brett, he said he wouldn't do it again and to the best of my knowledge he hasn't, and Brett's nightmares haven't returned since.

So how and why do spirits get earthbound? At some level they are attached to something or someone here. It may be a house they are particularly fond of, or a person. They are so attached they do not want to leave that place or person.

Their energy is low because they focus so much on what they are attached to on a physical level, rather than focusing internally. Were they to focus internally they would find themselves understanding their attachment to whatever it is and moving beyond those feelings into who they truly were. This experience of who they truly were would lift their resonance and they would go through quite naturally into spirit world. It is their fear of going within and feeling their feelings that manifests as a fear of moving on.

Other spirits come to help the spirits of people who have died to move over but sometimes the bond to the physical is stronger and that can keep them earthbound. Sometimes they fear moving on from this place because they fear that they will go to hell. In truth, there is no judgment day and there is no hell, but if you had it drummed into you as a child, would you trust a medium like me who you had not met before who told you 'it's okay to move on, there is no hell', or would you trust what had been drummed into you throughout your lifetime by people you knew? Some spirits can take a lot of persuading. It seems a fear of God or a fear of God's judgment has been instilled quite deeply in many people's psyches and that is rather sad, for God is Love. It is our minds, our thoughts and beliefs that create all the false fears, and left unchecked these false fears go on to manifest hell on earth for some people.

In Rob's case the biggest problem keeping him earthbound was his depressed low energy. He had needed a lot of energy over several days to help him to the stage where he now was. Andrew had talked to him at length to persuade him that he would not be judged, that even though he had chosen to end his own life he would not be punished. This can take a lot of believing for some spirits.

Rob felt like he was 'bad' and that he deserved to go to hell. He could see all the pain he had caused his family when he was alive and then even more when he took his own life without explanation. It took time and effort for Andrew to help him move over. Another male spirit who had taken his own life assisted in the process. This spirit was an old friend who was able to share with Rob a different perspective on suicide and reassure him that there would be no punishment and that there was no such place as hell. Rob was able to trust this close friend more readily than he could trust Andrew or me, and it was with this close friend's help that Rob did at last go home.

While all his energy and attention was focused into his life here, Rob was keeping himself locked into all the sadness and despair that he felt here. He was simply not able to forgive himself for all the pain he had caused and was still causing.

When he could start taking his focus off this life and turn it to what else might exist, his energies started to lift and he was at last able to return home. There he got to review his life and how each of his thoughts, actions and beliefs affected his experience of life and the lives of those around him. Not all his thoughts, actions and beliefs had had negative effects. From this broader perspective he could then make new choices about what he wanted to experience and learn on the next part of his journey. He would still be able to visit his physical family, but in a way that did not frighten his youngest son.

Andrew and I receive many requests, sometimes several a day, to assist with energies that are making the residents of a house uncomfortable, or spirits that are adversely affecting children. If you think that you may have a troublesome spirit in your home, your local church should be able to help them to move over. It's not something to try doing yourself unless you have had proper training.

One of the popular misconceptions is that troublesome spirits need to be sent towards the light. Even people who are quite experienced with spirit world can fall into this easy trap, because of what they have read in books, seen in movies, or in rare cases been taught.

Dawn was a medium whom I had met only once before. When we met for the second time I was quite surprised at how different she looked. Her hair and make-up were the same as I remembered, but she looked sort of grey. Perhaps she was ill, I thought to myself. I was sure she had looked very different the last time we had met.

It was a social meeting with others present and so I didn't like to draw attention to her 'greyness' but when she complained of feeling very lethargic, I became increasingly concerned. Dawn had described it as being due to overwork but I wasn't so sure.

I decided to take a peek at her psychically — not something I usually do because it feels a bit like being nosy and looking in someone's underwear drawer. I was glad I did. It looked like she had a large number of spirits in her space.

'Have you been doing much work helping spirits move over?' I asked, curious about what I was seeing in her auric space and about what could have caused this sudden deterioration in her physical condition.

'Yes I have,' she replied. 'What makes you ask?'

'You look like you have a lot of spirits in your space,' I explained.

'Well, I have been doing a lot of mediumship lately,' she said. On the surface it was a reasonable enough explanation but why would they still be hanging around?

'I am just wondering, have you found that the mediumship has been less clear of late?' I asked. She leaned a little closer to me.

'Yes I have,' she said, quite taken aback, 'but I think I have just been trying to do too much.'

'If you don't mind me asking, when you help spirits move over, what do you do?' I was sure that I was onto something. Her energetic field was filled with spirits; it was like looking at a nurse who tended the terminally ill. You can often spot nurses at the mediumship shows, because they are the ones with more spirits around them than anyone else.

Unless Dawn had lost a lot of loved ones very recently something was clearly not right. 'I just talk to them and send them into the light,' she said. 'Why do you ask?'

We didn't know each other very well and so perhaps I was overstepping the mark but I did feel I knew what was wrong and our paths certainly seemed to be crossing for a reason. Her answer had confirmed my suspicions.

'Have you ever thought that when you do that you may be the lightest thing in the room, and that you are inviting the spirits into you?'

Her face fell. I could see she hadn't even considered that before. She was doing what she had been taught by another medium, but in light of her present tiredness she was now wide open to the idea that it could be spirits causing this level of lethargy.

Now I had her interest and her curiosity. The lack of clarity with her mediumship had been a worry to her. It was how she made her living and she couldn't afford to have a 'foggy head', as she called it.

'What do you do when you help souls to pass over?' she asked with interest.

'First I invite Christ to be present. That sets up protection for all concerned and helps us all feel safe. Most of the spirits I have had to deal with have had some kind of Christian background. Then I ask the spirit if they would like to go home. We may need to talk for a while but when they are ready to go home I ask Christ to open up the appropriate doorway for them.

'I ask that all they have learned here be honoured, for every life has value, and I ask that all their learning be shared with the whole. Then I observe them as they move out of this dimension and I send them love and light for their onward journey. Not all spirits are made of "light" — some would literally be terrified of going into the light. It would show up the pain (darkness) that they hold far too strongly. Such spirits need to go through to a dimension that is comfortable for them and that means a place where the energy is similar to how they are currently vibrating. To you or I that may look dark, but to them it is what they are familiar and comfortable with.'

'So what should I do now to help the spirits that are still in my space move over?'

'It's the same process, but it is perhaps easier if someone else says the words and then you can concentrate on how you are feeling. We can do it later today if you like.'

Dawn didn't want to wait — she was fed up with feeling so tired all the time.

'Can we nip out now? My home is only a few doors away,' she said.

'Sure.' We made our excuses and headed over to her place.

The process took us about twenty minutes or so. At the end of it Dawn was feeling more like her old self and all the greyness had lifted.

'I can't believe how much better I feel!' she exclaimed as the last spirit left. 'Thank heavens you knew what was wrong with me. I could have gone on like that picking up more and more spirits.'

'Sooner or later your health would have suffered,' I said, 'and that would have stopped you from taking on any more. The signs are easy to spot when you know what you are looking for. There is an unwarranted tiredness and a greyness in how the person looks. I can only recognise it because I have been there too.'

Talking about my own experience levelled the playing field again. It helped our friendship for her to know that I had made the same mistake too a few years before.

I knew that Dawn wouldn't ever fall into the same trap again and that in addition she would be able to recognise the signs in others whose paths crossed with her own. It gave me a lovely warm feeling to know that the sharing of this knowledge would ripple out through her and affect many others, and to feel that this shared knowledge had already brought us closer.

6. Losing a Child

'Getting up each day. That is the hardest thing for me to do.'

The tension was almost unbearable. I hardly dared to breathe, as though something as slight as a breath would make this young lady let go of the cobweb-fine threshold that was holding all her emotions in check. I sat silently witnessing and accepting her pain.

Sabina, the mother of a two-year-old who had passed away in a tragic accident, had a depth of pain that I had not seen before. It was a pain that I could barely even comprehend. Every part of her body ached with the pain of losing her precious daughter Ellie. Every cell wanted to hold her just one last time.

As I sat with Sabina I knew that it would not

take much at all for this exterior to just crumple and all the emotions tumble out once more. I sat with her for what seemed like an eternity, feeling her pain. A family photograph caught my attention out of the corner of my eye. I could see from the photograph that this lovely young woman had aged something like ten years in the past twelve months. From how she now felt it was obvious that it wasn't getting any easier for her, or Dad, her stalwart in all of this.

It was the wider family that had asked for my help and had approached me first through a family friend. I had been wary about seeing Mum (Sabina) at first as I didn't want to add to her pain — and that was entirely possible if I couldn't get a meaningful communication from her daughter. From what the family had told me it was still extremely difficult for Sabina to even talk about her daughter, who had died the previous year.

Now I could see why the family had been so desperate. Sabina was morose, and not handling her daughter's passing at all well. She was in a place where few would be able to access her, and in that place she was cutting herself off from her other children. She was doing this in two ways: energetically, because all her energy was pulled in protectively around her; and physically, because she seemed to be in her head all the time and did not respond as sensitively as she had done to their day-to-day needs. Doctors had prescribed medication for

Sabina, but it hadn't seemed to help.

Sabina had been in charge of Ellie when she ran onto the road. Mum had turned her back to pick up groceries that had fallen out of a torn carrier bag and those few seconds had been all it took. She had let go of Ellie's hand just for an instant, taken her eyes off her only for seconds. She had heard a woman scream out and lifted her head in time to hear the thud of the van hitting Ellie. She knew it had hit her daughter, she just knew it.

There hadn't even been time for the driver to brake. Ellie's body had taken the full impact of the van. It's a scene many parents fear. For Sabina it had become a sharp, intense reality. With her own eyes she had seen her child's broken body lying in the road. There had been nothing that anyone could do. Ellie had been killed outright. Sabina had held her daughter's warm, limp body as the paramedics arrived, fervently praying that somehow, some way, Ellie could be brought back to life. At the hospital she had been sedated for her own well-being.

Now Mum blamed herself. What was she thinking, to let go of her hand and give her attention to groceries, of all things? She knew it was a busy corner and that Ellie didn't yet know about crossing roads. In her eyes there was no excuse for what had happened. She wanted for it all not to have happened. At times she wanted to die, partly because of the remorse she felt and partly because that way she would be with Ellie.

Ellie had been two and a half, that wonderful age when youngsters can tell you that they are two and a half. It was how she introduced herself to complete strangers.

'Everyone loved her,' Sabina said, choking back the tears. 'Especially the boys.'

Ellie had been a much longed-for daughter after three boys. Every day with her had been precious and the boys had enjoyed their new sister as much as Mum and Dad had. She had brought a new energy into the household: a gentleness and delightful, playful giggles.

'I miss her so much. I wish I could just turn the clock back or wake up from this. It hurts so much.'

I nodded as Sabina went on.

'It was my fault. I should have been more careful. She knew not to go onto the road but we think she saw a cat on the other side. At least that is what a passerby had witnessed. A lady saw her, saw it all happening and screamed out. I just couldn't get to her in time, no one could.'

Sabina was rocking gently back and forth as she replayed the events again for what must have been the thousandth or millionth time.

'The driver couldn't see her above the parked cars. It wasn't his fault. He was only a young man but it really wasn't his fault. I should have been closer to her.'

The self-inflicted torture continued.

'The young man was shaking. I don't think he

will ever get over it. I didn't expect her to run out like that. There was no warning. I couldn't get to her in time.'

Sabina's eyes were downcast. She was really in her pain now, really feeling it. I could understand why her family wanted help for her. It would be difficult to witness someone you love going through this day after day.

Medication left her feeling, in her words, like a zombie. It was important to Sabina that her lack of attention didn't cause harm to any of her other children and yet here she was in her pain, not able to function properly. She was so numb and tired from the pain of it all. I wondered how long it had been since she had slept well.

'How are you finding sleeping?' I gently inquired when there was a suitable pause.

'I'm not,' she said sighing, 'except when I take the sleeping tablets from the doctor, but I don't like taking them because I feel so groggy the next day.'

I nodded in understanding. I have only ever had a sleeping pill once myself but have heard this description from many who have taken them.

'Would you like me to see if I can get Ellie through?' I wasn't sure if that was what she wanted, or just to talk.

Sabina nodded.

Sometimes when the emotion is so intense it is really difficult to make and sustain a link with spirit world as the coarser, heavier emotions can block out the higher, finer frequencies of a loving communication. I took a deep breath and allowed myself to relax.

Thankfully Ellie's communication was not impeded by all the emotion. Ellie was a mass of giggling golden-blonde curls. She came through with her paternal great-grandmother, Nell.

Ellie was very playful, as she was here. She named two of her brothers, the two whose names she had mastered while in this physical life, and gave the nickname she had created for the third. She had been camping with them, she told me proudly, sticking out her two-and-a-half-year-old chest. Mum confirmed that the boys had been camping just the weekend before with their grandfather. It wasn't something they usually did and there had been a lot of excitement about spending the night under the stars.

A tear rolled down Mum's cheek. Her daughter really was all right and she was spending time with her brothers. She was so pleased that Ellie was still around and a part of the family.

'She has her kitten,' I told her. 'It's a little black one.'

'She didn't have a kitten,' said Mum, momentarily taken aback.

'Ellie is showing me a kitten, a tiny black kitten. It died like she did.'

Mum was sobbing again. When she was calmer she managed to explain to me that their cat had kittens the previous year. Each boy was allowed to keep one as Mum and Dad thought it would help them get over Ellie's death and allow them to feel again, and yes, the runt of the litter, a black one, had died. It hadn't even been named and it ended up causing even more distress to the boys.

'Destiny,' I was told by Ellie, and it struck me as a very odd name for a two-and-a-half-year-old to give a kitten. But of course the spirit within Ellie had lived many times before. Ellie called the kitten Destiny because it was always destined to be with her. I felt that Ellie was trying to convey to Mum that sometimes things happen in life that we do not want to happen, but always there is an underlying reason that we may not understand.

The boys did not want the little black kitten to die; it was the cutest one, being so small. But its passing allowed them to cry once more and to grieve again for Ellie, and Ellie got to have a kitten of her own. It was the youngest kitten, as she had been the youngest of their family. There were many parallels when we started talking about it. Little by little the bigger picture was starting to emerge.

Mum wanted to know if any of the boys saw Ellie, so I asked her.

Ellie shook her head and then showed me how they talked about her a lot and usually that was when she was around: she popped into their thoughts.

'How are your brothers?' I asked Ellie in my head. She smiled. She gave me the feeling that the older brothers were moving on, although the youngest still got tearful at times, but on the whole they were doing well. Mum confirmed that was her view too.

I hadn't asked about Dad but Ellie went on to show me that Dad in his own way was coping as men often do, busying himself with work and the upbringing of the boys. Mum was the one who was stuck in a place the family and Ellie were finding it increasingly hard to access. The feeling was that Sabina should be feeling less pain, not more, and that somehow she had got stuck.

'Misplaced guilt' popped into my head and not from Ellie but from Nell, Ellie's great-grandmother who until then had stood back. I knew instinctively that it was guilt that was keeping Sabina from moving on — but how to tackle this? Internally I asked for help.

'Please give me the words I need to help Sabina move on.'

The response came swiftly.

'Ellie is worried about you,' I conveyed in as caring a manner as I could. 'She says you aren't like you used to be. You used to be so much fun, so smiley. She is sorry you are feeling so much pain. She knows you don't understand why she had to die, why she had to leave your beautiful family and why you had to be the one to see what happened to her physical body.'

There was a pause and then: 'She loves you so

much.' I held Sabina's hand and continued.

'She knows that one of the obstacles to you accepting what has happened is your guilt. That you feel responsible for her death. You are not responsible for her death. She is.'

I could sense an altogether more powerful presence speaking through me. It was a calming, peaceful presence and was assured of the truth of its knowingness.

'A soul cannot leave the physical realm except of its own free will. That choice may not be made consciously on a physical level but it is made with the full consciousness of the incarnating soul.'

The words coming through me were strong, powerful and matter of fact. I could feel my ego resisting them — how could Ellie choose this and do this to her brothers, her family and her mother? This was hurting Mum so much.

The words coming out of me, although beautifully expressed, still seemed very harsh. I didn't see how they would help. The wise soul speaking through me was absolutely assured that this had been Ellie's choice.

'Why would she choose to leave such a loving family?' I found myself screaming in my head. 'Why would she choose to cause so much pain?'

'I didn't choose to cause the pain. That is caused by the attachment to a painful belief, one that the family is holding.' I was still hearing from Ellie, but from a higher aspect of herself, the part that understood what was going on. 'I have had many physical incarnations and I did not need to reincarnate again on the earth but I chose to. I chose to help my brothers and sisters (and I knew she included Mum and Dad in this description) understand how they cause themselves pain. How the beliefs that they hold are not truly real. When a belief becomes too painful to hold onto eventually you have to let it go. The family holds a belief in death and a belief in separation. It is the holding onto this belief that causes the pain.'

I was pretty much speechless. What Ellie said made sense although I really wasn't at all sure that Mum was ready to hear this, but what had been said had been said. It was what Ellie had wanted to say. Before I had a chance to check how Mum was feeling, Ellie was drawing my attention to another little girl with her in spirit world. It was her cousin. I couldn't get a name but I knew that the two girls were very close in age.

Sabina was a little lost for a moment, which was hardly surprising given the communication that had just come from her daughter. I could see her mentally struggling to take in not only what had been said but also to recognise who this cousin was that Ellie was talking about. While Mum looked perplexed I asked for more information. I was shown a girl the same age as Ellie, but who had passed away as a baby.

Of course. The penny dropped. Sabina realised that it must be the baby her sister-in-law had lost while she was carrying Ellie. They had been pregnant at the same time. The realisation hit her like a ton of bricks. She had not thought about what her sister-in-law had gone through miscarrying her baby — she had been so wrapped up in her own pain.

I could see the news that the two girls were together was shaking Sabina's world. Someone else had been through what she had been through, albeit with a different set of circumstances — someone else knew how she felt. All of a sudden she realised that she had not known how her sister-in-law felt until now. At the time she had told her how sorry she was, but in lots of ways these had been empty words for she did not *know* until now.

Sabina still hurt and felt numb and disconnected, but she also understood now what others go through when they lose a child. For the first time Sabina glimpsed how Ellie's death had helped her to change. It wasn't going to make the pain of losing Ellie any less. She would miss her every day of her life, but at some level she could see that she had grown through the experience, that it wasn't all bad, and that Ellie's passing could in time help her to connect with others even more deeply.

Until then, it was time she talked with her sister-in-law. She realised she had been thinking only of herself and her own pain, and now that she knew what her sister-in-law had been going through too, she wanted to help because she knew how much it hurt.

There was just one question Sabina had for me before I left.

'Why can't I see her like you do?'

'Seeing can be difficult because our logical brain kicks in,' I explained. 'You do sense her though, don't you? And smell her?'

Sabina confirmed she did on both counts.

'Work with that. Be open to sensing her. When you wake up each morning say to yourself: "Wouldn't it be wonderful to sense Ellie around today" — and you will. Every time she pops into your head she's around.'

'She must be around an awful lot,' Sabina said, managing a half smile.

'She is.' I smiled back.

'It will do you a lot of good to talk about how you are feeling with your sister-in-law. It really helps to know that someone else is going through what we are going through. The circumstances may be very different but we do tend to have the same kinds of feelings come up. I think you will both be able to help each other. You may also want to find out what bereavement support is available for you.'

'The doctor suggested that to me before but I didn't think it would help,' Sabrina replied.

'It will,' I gently reaffirmed.

Sabina didn't miraculously recover and get on with her life. We don't. But she did find the next step on her journey: reaching out to her sister-in-law. She still has a long way to go. Grieving takes as long as it takes. Mediumship can help when a person is stuck in the process.

For me, the most painful messages I have to deliver are from the children.
The children themselves are fine — they are free of their physical pain, they know they do not die. The pain rests with those who are left behind. How do you make that better? Perhaps my work is not about making things better, for there will always be the pain of loss on a physical level. Perhaps instead my work is about helping people understand why they are in so much pain and helping them let go of beliefs about this reality that not only cause them pain but limit their experience of this life.

I was at a mind, body and spirit festival when one of my guides decided to talk through me at a public talk. This is called channelling. Instead of allowing a spirit to talk through me I allow a higher non-physical intelligence to talk through me. This is a spirit that is very evolved, a spiritual teacher that can help us to understand more about this reality because they hold a higher perspective. On this occasion I had handed over to Elim, one of my guides, and he was talking to a large group about the nature of this physical reality. At the end of his talk Elim invited questions. The question of a young dark-haired girl held the audience's attention. It was perhaps a question they all wanted to ask.

'When you die do you get to see all your relatives that have already died?'

'My dear,' said Elim speaking through me, 'you will love the answer to this question, for you get to see not only those who have died but those who are still alive.'

The auditorium was silent as the significance of Elim's words filtered through. In my head I was getting quite agitated: what did he mean? But Elim was in charge and was intent on completing the teaching he had started.

'When you dream at night, where do you think you go?' Elim asked almost teasingly. It was a rhetorical question. No one responded and Elim's teaching went on to explain that this reality is the dream and that we experience more of our true nature when we are sleeping, but we call that 'dreaming'. Elim found it hilarious that we called our true self state 'dreaming' and called the real dream 'reality'.

According to Elim we dream ourselves into this reality each day. The concept took some comprehending and yet at some level it all felt true. I felt that just my mind couldn't understand it. Elim described the mind as a cage that we do not realise we are locked in. He said that we think we are experiencing life but really we are only experiencing the filters of our own minds, our own cages. We needed to step out of our own cages to know and understand the nature of true self. (There will be more from Elim in the future. He exists in a state of being consciousness; without attachments to personality likes and dislikes; in a pure, blissful state of being; and he helps me to step outside the square of my own thinking at times.)

In the days after Elim's unexpected teaching there was a dawning realisation within me: when we die, we get to see all those who have gone before and those who are still in our lives.

In dream state I had seen my father when he was much younger, with a full head of hair and in his true nature — and he hadn't died. Over the years I have seen in dreams both the living and those who have died. In my twelve years as a medium spirits have *never* told their loved ones, through me, that they miss them. What Elim had said was ringing bells.

I know that when I work as a medium my brain goes into a different state. My head is clear and yet relaxed. Researchers call this an 'alpha' state. It is a focused and aware state, in which the brainwaves run at about eight to twelve cycles per second compared with the 'normal' thirteen to twenty-five cycles per second — the 'beta' state. The 'beta' state is what we are usually in as we go about our daily lives. At the other end of the spectrum is the 'theta' state, when the cycles are much lower and we experience deep sleep.

It is most common for us to experience 'aha' or enlightenment moments in 'alpha' state and it is also very common for people to see their spirit-world loved-ones just as they are falling into or awakening from sleep. It makes sense to me then that spirit world can most easily be experienced on this frequency.

Elim's teaching was starting to make sense, but I knew that I still needed my own experiences of what he was saying before I could accept it as my truth.

7. Why Do Spirits Communicate with Us?

Over the years I have found that there are lots of different, individual reasons why loved ones in spirit world communicate with us, but there are also some common themes. In this chapter I share with you some of the more significant reasons.

Sometimes it is to make amends for what has happened in the past, as this next story shows.

Robert, the father I brought through for his daughter, was very sorry. So very, very sorry.

Since Robert had passed into the spiritual dimensions he had been given the opportunity to review his life and had seen how his behaviour had affected so many different aspects of his daughter's life. He told me he had been over in spirit world about six of our years.

I wasn't sure that this was a message I could convey in front of an audience, because the daughter might get very distressed. I didn't know yet what Dad was wanting to apologise for — it could be emotional abuse, physical abuse or worse. I wasn't at all sure that this should be dealt with in front of a public audience but Dad persisted. He was adamant about making amends.

Dad's remorse was almost tangible, and as I approached his daughter I could feel all the words welling up inside me, waiting to spill out. There was so much he needed to say.

'I have your dad with me in spirit world,' I said to the young, fair-haired lady in front of me. 'He's been over about six years.'

'Six and a half,' she said, nodding.

'He is really, really sorry,' I conveyed. She just looked at me, tears welling in her eyes. Yes, I would have to leave it to the end of the show. I wasn't being shown sexual abuse but there was still a lot of pain here and she was not that old, maybe twenty-two or twenty-three, and it wouldn't be right to do this one publicly.

Her name was Tamlyn. We both agreed it would be best to see each other after the show. This initial approach to his daughter appeased Dad and he stood back so that I was able to proceed with other messages for the audience.

At the end of the show Tamlyn and I found a quiet corner together and Dad was able to say what he had been wanting to say for so long.

'I am sorry for how I treated you,' he said, full of emotion. 'I should have encouraged you more. I didn't. I am sorry.'

Inside he showed me that — more than the words he used — it had been his manner with his daughter, the disdainful looks, ignoring her when a few words of encouragement would have made a world of difference. He had been wrapped up in himself during his lifetime, and he had never really given a thought as to how this had affected Tamlyn, his only child. He hadn't been happy here, he could see that now. He was not happy because the choices he made were not what he really wanted and he didn't have the courage to make different choices. When he reflected on his life he could see that his lack of happiness was not Tamlyn's fault, and that he had taken his unhappiness out on her while he was here.

Now in the spirit world he had realised that he could not recall a single time when he had ever said to her, 'Well done!' — and that had been a shocking realisation for him. He had always considered himself a good father. Yes, he had provided for his daughter, but he had not been there for her.

Tamlyn had learned to praise and encourage herself but it had also made her hard, hard in a way that was not helpful to her ongoing development.

He could see this now and he didn't want her to harden as he had. Tamlyn needed to know she was okay, that she was more than okay, that she was his daughter and that he was so very proud of her. He was especially sorry about the piano. She had taken it up as a child and he had stopped her from playing. He wished he hadn't.

Auntie Alice was with him and I conveyed this. Tamlyn couldn't quite understand the link with Auntie Alice at first as she was on Mum's side of the family. I asked for help and was again shown the piano.

'The link is the piano,' I said, hoping it would shed more light on the connection.

It turned out that Tamlyn had inherited her Auntie Alice's piano within the last year. It was Dad's way of affirming that she should continue to learn to play.

'I'm too old now,' she said, pulling a face.

'Dad doesn't think so. You have a real musical talent — one he wishes he had encouraged.'

Tamlyn agreed she had loved music but hadn't ever thought about herself as having any talents in that area.

'Dad's wanting you to do what you love and not make the mistakes he did. You are never too old to start making better choices.'

This she could relate to. Dad had not made good choices. Inaction and indifference had been his choice.

That night Dad had made a better choice. He had chosen to come through and show her that he cared. He had chosen to encourage her and take an interest in her life. The love link between them could only be strengthened by this decision.

Overnight I was given a further insight that has a more universal application: only we know what it is we love or have a passion for. No one else does. It is we who need to make the choices to follow our heartfelt desires. No one else can do this for us — it is our responsibility.

Dad knew that whether Tamlyn followed her heart or not would be up to Tamlyn. He just felt he had not been a good example for her. His life had been one of not following his heart. He felt he had then made matters worse by squashing her musical dreams many moons ago when he stopped her from doing what she loved — playing the piano. Dad wanted to make amends for that and give her a gentle push back in the direction of her dreams, encouraging her to follow her heart, with his blessing.

For me personally, there was also another insight. It doesn't take a lot to encourage a child in something they are interested in or have an ability for. I made a mental note to watch for the signs in my own children, and to encourage them in the direction of their own hearts, as their paths may differ significantly from my own. What feels right for me may well not feel right for them and as I trust them to follow their own hearts, their confidence in doing this will grow. If they are always looking to me for what feels right they will stop using their own internal guidance system, and then when I am not there they will be at a loss for what to do. It was an important insight.

Sometimes the messages that come through can take the recipients by surprise. What they think is important turns out not to be, as this next example shows.

The communication was done backstage as Dad had been murdered and it was quite a public case. In a way I was amazed that the family had come to the show as they would have known that they would be recognised in such a small town. They had come not because they needed to know that Dad was okay but because they needed to talk with me about Dad's ashes. Each of the daughters had had their own experiences with Dad since he had passed away. One had heard Dad call her name, another had seen him in a dream and the youngest sensed him with her regularly.

They all knew in their own way that Dad was okay, but the problem in their eyes was Dad's ashes. Dad had remarried just four years before his death and it had caused a huge rift in the family. His daughters and their children, his grandchildren, had hardly seen him. When he died so suddenly the ashes passed to his new wife, Gemma. The daughters were distraught — the ashes were all they had left of him and they had been taken from them. What could they do?

Dad, when he came through, was a really matter-of-fact guy. A rough diamond I guess some would call him. A hard man in lots of ways, but he had found a way into his daughters' hearts and they into his.

'Tell them it's not about the ashes,' Dad said to me almost immediately. 'It's about what the ashes represent.'

He didn't wait long before he continued: 'It's me they are mad at really, not Gemma. They feel I turned my back on them and I did. They have every right to be angry.'

The family was silent but I could see that what Dad was saying was ringing true.

'I didn't mean to shut them out. I felt guilty. Guilty for what I had done to their mother, my wife. Seeing them made me feel bad because of the guilt I carried. Their mother stood by me through thick and thin and I wasn't an easy bugger to live with, I can tell you.'

'That's Dad.' One of the daughters smiled. It was clear Dad's message was getting through.

'It's me they miss — that's what hurts — not those god-forsaken ashes. I couldn't give a stuff about the ashes. That's not what is important. It's about them and me. Nothing can get in the way of us again, nothing: not Gemma, not my guilt, not their anger, not death, nothing.'

All agreed Dad had not changed much at all on the spirit world side of life. He still told it like it was, using the colourful language that they all remembered so well. Just as well he hadn't come through in public, I thought to myself. I would have needed to bleep out every other word. After the communication with him, the ashes just weren't that important after all — they knew they had his love and they knew that each of them had an internal connection with him that could never, ever, be taken from them.

Sometimes a message heals us in a way therapy can't, as this next story shows.

Denise asked for a word with me after a show.

'I really don't like to trouble you. I am not usually someone who would ask this because you do look so tired but I have been to two of your shows hoping my dad would come through and he hasn't. I wondered if you had any message for me?'

My head was pounding. I wasn't expecting her dad to come through quite so quickly.

He had shot himself, I just knew it. She had been only a child. How can you not respond when you see something like that? I was tired but I just melted.

'Did your Dad take his own life?' I asked cautiously. She nodded. I let her know he was with me and said that I would do what I could, but she would need to wait until everyone else had gone. She was happy to wait.

Alan, her father, was back with me as soon as the last person had left. He had gone into the attic and shot himself.

She nodded. She just wanted to understand why. Why did he feel the need to do that? It was an understandable question.

Inside I could feel how he felt, and I experienced visually what he had experienced.

'He could not live with his thoughts. Black thoughts,' I said.

I knew the words I was using were inadequate to describe what I was seeing. He had been sexually abused by a man, an uncle I felt it was. So what should I do? Pass on what I was shown or would this add to this poor girl's pain? I asked for guidance from my own guides. 'The truth will out' came into my head.

I carefully conveyed what I had seen, noticing how she was responding to what I described. It was not news to her. The 'uncle' had been a boyfriend of his mother's. Denise told me that her mother had shared a similar account with her. Dad had battled depression for so many years. He found it very hard to live with the memories in his head, day in and day out, seeing the pictures, reliving the physical pain. He had needed surgery to repair some of the damage. It was because of these terrible images that he had made the conscious choice to end his life. It hadn't been a spur-of-the-moment choice — it had been a thought-through decision. He was sorry if his decision had hurt her but he really couldn't go on with that level of torture in his head day and night. He hoped that Denise would understand and forgive him.

I felt very uncomfortable conveying the message and talking about such things but it turned out to be just what Denise needed to hear. As painful as it was, the message brought relief and closure on both sides.

Dad hadn't taken his life because his life with Mum and Denise was unhappy; it was because of the images he had in his head, and now he was free of them. Denise had heard this version of accounts from Mum already, but somehow hearing it from Dad gave her the peace she so desperately needed. She knew her dad would still have been battling his demons here if he had remained in a physical body, but in spirit world he could at last be at peace. Denise could finally move on.

Sometimes, though it is much rarer, our loved ones come through to tell us off for not seeing what they can see so plainly.

Sandra and Dave had invited me to their home. They had lost their little boy just two years before and I had helped them come to terms with their loss the previous year. They had called me because they felt they needed help once more. Sandra had arranged the meeting.

'It's not Daddy's fault,' were the first words out of my mouth. Jayden, their eight-year-old, was talking through me. Before I had time to think, Mum exploded.

'Well I don't know whose fault it is if it's not Daddy's!'

Wow. I had walked right into the middle of this one. No prior warning. Life has taught me not to get in the middle of an arguing couple — when they make up it is always going to be your fault. You don't take sides. My brain was thinking one thing and my mouth was doing another.

'You weren't letting Daddy get close to you. You shut him out,' came out before I could stop it. I was arguing with a lady who had lost her child. I was supposed to be helping her, not shouting at her. Jayden had the upper hand and he was not letting Mummy get away with this. Mummy was not going to blame Daddy for this — it was down to both of them.

Mummy was getting a telling-off and Daddy was looking mighty guilty and more than a little relieved that I hadn't turned on him.

'Do you know what he's done?' Mum spluttered at me. She didn't have to tell me. Her son already had. Dad had found comfort in the arms of another woman, a friend of Mum's.

'After all we've been through,' she said in despair.

Dad looked sheepish and stayed very quiet, which incidentally is a very good strategy at times like this. All I could think was: well, this man has balls — he must have known what he was letting himself in for, coming to this meeting. I was working desperately hard not to judge the situation.

Jayden was not taking sides, although it could have appeared like that at first. Instead he was evening up the playing field, by telling it like it was.

'You wouldn't open up to Daddy, you wouldn't connect with him, so he found someone who could.'

Jayden showed me that to move through our feelings we need to feel them, and that connecting with others during this time can deepen and enrich our connection with our feelings. Jayden wanted his passing to bring them closer, not push them further apart. If Mum continued to blame Dad for all of this, they would end up separating and none of the hurt would get healed. That wasn't what this was all about. Mum had to accept the part she had played in all of this.

The situation was not irreparable. Dad genuinely regretted his mistake. He was here, wasn't he, putting himself though all this? He hadn't walked away: he had been honest about his mistake and was hanging in there trying to make it all right.

Mum, she was mad. Not just mad at Dad, mad at her so-called 'friend' who had played a part in this situation, mad about losing her child and just plain mad at God. And from her perspective, didn't she have every right to be?

Jayden had matched her energy and taken the wind out of her sails. He had Mum's attention. Even I was taken aback by what was coming out of my mouth. As a woman I would perhaps have sided with Mum — how awful that her husband would do this to her, and at a time like this. But Jayden's speech had stopped me completely in my tracks. His was a different perspective — and we were all attentive to what he had to say.

It takes two people to make a connection. As human beings we need our connection with each other. We know instinctively when someone shuts us out. We sense it. In this case the shutting-out had been not only energetically but also on the more obvious physical level. Mum had physically pushed Dad away at times. She didn't deny this.

Dad had needed someone to talk to, to work through his feelings with, and he had turned to a family friend. Mum couldn't talk at that time; she was still hurting too much. She wasn't deliberately shutting Dad out — it was just her way of coping. Dad's way of coping was to talk to someone. As he started to talk and open up again he happened to open up to the wrong person, a person of the opposite sex, and an energetic connection formed between them. He found himself thinking about her and he started to fall in love. He knew that it felt wrong at the time, but it felt less wrong than keeping in all the hurt, which he had been doing so far.

'Nothing has prepared me for this,' I remembered Dad sobbing at our first meeting to talk to Jayden. He was so right. We aren't taught how to lose a loved one or how to grieve. None of us knows how we will react until we lose someone close. We may do things we wouldn't normally do. We may regret the things we do, but each of us is always doing the best we can and we shouldn't ever forget that. There are far worse things in life than having someone be unfaithful to us — as anyone who has lost a child will confirm. That doesn't make it right, it just puts it into perspective — what is important here: moving on and loving again, or holding onto past hurts?

It's a choice we get to make again and again in life — and Jayden was calling his parents on it. Yes, Dad had made a mistake. A big mistake. Yes, he had hurt Mum, but he really didn't mean to. He was just trying to process his own emotions and find himself again. He made a mistake, not a mistake he was ever likely to make again, but if this situation was to be resolved he and Mum would both have to let him off the hook for this. If they did not, the barriers between them would become insurmountable. A big mistake would be turned into a huge one, hurting Jayden's brothers and sisters, and Jayden *really* didn't want that to happen.

To put it another way, Jayden was challenging

his Mum and Dad to think about whether their actions and reactions were taking them towards reconciliation or into a battle. What was it they wanted? You can't truly want peace while you are standing there drawing everyone's attention to all the ammunition the other has just hurled at you. If you truly want peace you let go of what has happened; you create a space in which the two of you can connect once more and heal past hurts.

The ball was in Mum's and Dad's court now. Jayden had said his piece — or should it be 'peace'? His loving energy started to withdraw. He was one mighty feisty eight-year-old. One who loved his Mum and Dad and brothers and sisters with a passion.

Jayden's message also gave a more universal insight into why it may be that some people are drawn into affairs — perhaps they get pulled in looking for an energetic connection with another, when what they really need is a better connection with their existing partner, or themselves, or with God.

Whatever the message, whatever the circumstances, there is always an underlying theme for a spirit-world communication.

From spirit world, in their true self state, our loved ones can see that part of us is stuck in this physical reality because of a perspective that we hold. That part of us, which is ignorant about their survival in spirit form, is trapped, stuck in the pain that is created by the illusion of our perspective. Our loved ones come through in their true self state to help release us from the illusions we hold. For they know that if the perspective can be seen for what it is, the illusion that is causing the pain will be shattered once and for all. It might be a perspective about who we are, about how we are causing ourselves or another pain, or about how we are limiting ourselves. Whatever the perspective is, if it is flawed it needs correcting — and spirit world can and does help us to do this again and again.

HELP IS AT HAND

*I see you walking on the beach but you do
    not see me.
I see you slipping off your shoes and gazing
    out to sea,
The sunlight on the water dances to and fro,
I'm sensing your aloneness, the hurt you
    won't let go.
The seagulls flying overhead let out a
    playful cry,
I watch you as you watch them and then
    I hear you sigh.
You think there is nowhere to turn, there is
    no help at hand,*

*Yet here we are, your guardians, barefoot on
   the sand.*
*A tear rolls down one angel's cheek,
   another holds your hand,*
*We feel the things you're feeling, we truly
   understand.*
*You hug your jacket closer, and we embrace
   you too,*
*If you could only see us, we would surely
   help you through*
*The days ahead without the one you loved
   so very much.*
*My child, it pains us deeply that you cannot
   feel our touch.*
*Your loved one is among us now, safe in
   our embrace,*
*They watch you as you go through life and
   gently touch your face,*
*Your loved one can't be seen by you and so
   wants you to know,*
*How much they truly loved you; they wish
   they'd told you so.*
*How every time you think of them they're
   with you as you cry,*
*How wonderful this life is when you find
   you do not die!*

8. A New Perspective on Suicide

I first saw Shaun very briefly as I awoke. He looked to be about fifteen or sixteen years of age with short, dark hair cropped close to his head. He had an awkward, self-conscious sort of smile that many teenagers have and that in its own way was quite appealing. I was due to see a lady and her husband later that day and I already knew that they had lost their son. I was glad he had 'popped in' in advance — it helped me to relax for the rest of the day knowing that when the time came he would be able to come through.

Mum was much younger than I had expected — about my own age. Because I have had my own children quite late in life and they are still young, six and eight, I sometimes forget that people my own age can have older children.

Mum and Dad introduced themselves and after only a few minutes of small talk we made our way through into the lounge. I saw no sense in delaying. They had already waited long enough, and what they wanted was to talk to their son.

I could tell that Mum and Dad, although very keen to hear from their son, were perhaps a little uncomfortable. I consider myself and my home very ordinary, and hope that this helps put people at ease, but when you haven't seen a medium before and you want to talk to a much-loved son it can be quite nerve-wracking.

It's best not to have long silences at times like this as they can add to the tension. Fortunately we didn't have to wait long for the spiritual link with their son.

I had meant to sit in a chair but instead found myself sitting on the floor at Mum's feet. Why? I asked. Why sit here?

I usually sit alongside the people I see and this different sitting position had taken me by surprise. Physically I knew he was showing me he was her son, placing himself lower than her, smaller than her, looking up to her.

There was something else he wanted to show me and that was his connection with her, how beautiful it was, a soft gentle energy that would forever hold the two together. He had to move his consciousness away from Mum and into my energetic space before he would be able to talk with me successfully. It took just a few seconds before I could feel him more fully with me.

I felt him as a youthful and yet wise being. I felt he was a young man who had taken this life and himself very seriously. No sooner had he connected with me energetically than a stream of information started flowing into my consciousness. He started with his name.

'He is showing me a short name, five or six letters, starting with an S.' I knew there was also a U — but when I asked him, 'Is it Stuart?', he indicated very firmly 'NO.'

'I don't know what his name is,' I said to his parents. 'He has shown me the S and that it also has a 'U' but I do know it's not Stuart — he has said "no" to that suggestion.'

In my head I saw my cousin Susan's face — her name had an S and a U in it but that wasn't a guy's name, so I dismissed it as my own mind trying to make sense of the letters.

'His name is Shaun,' Mum volunteered before I had the chance to ask for further information.

Aha, the penny dropped — my cousin Susan's husband at the time was called Shaun, that was why my guides had started to show me her face. Perhaps I should have let them continue. As it was, Mum had told me her son's name now and it was clear that for her and Dad I had been close enough.

Next Shaun showed me his grandmother with him in spirit world. She was Mum's mum, and she was a lovely lady. There was something about a connection they had, albeit briefly, and the anniversary of a passing.

Mum confirmed that Shaun had been a baby of just four months when his grandmother died but they had had time to bond. Mum had taken him over to Switzerland to meet his maternal grandmother just before she died. It had recently been the anniversary of her passing.

Shaun showed me details of Mum's work and other bits and pieces that would help both his parents and I know without doubt that I was talking to their much-loved son.

As I felt Shaun's spirit within me it was as though he was reflecting on the different aspects of his life here. As he carefully spoke through me I was very aware that he was really focusing his attention on Mum and that my eyes had barely left her for a second. It was clear that the love he had for both his parents was very deep, they had been wonderful parents to him, but at this time he knew it was Mum that most needed his help. He just wanted her to understand.

'Understand what?' I asked curiously.

While I waited patiently for his response I conveyed the other smaller, but significant, details that Shaun was passing on to me. When spirits talk with us they use telepathy, and information can come in on many different channels at once: words, pictures, feelings, smells, sensations, tastes and knowings.

With words and pictures Shaun was showing the smaller details of his life; it was rather like piecing together a mosaic. With a sense of deep knowing he was conveying a more important concept to me. It was a concept that my logical brain couldn't fathom. He was conveying to me that he had taken his own life deliberately, that he felt this was something he needed to do. When I challenged him on this point of view he told me he had taken his own life because it was his life path, his purpose.

When we try to make sense of new concepts or information, very often what the mind does is try to understand the new concept by aligning it with something we have already experienced or learned about. We try to fit the new piece of information into our existing framework of beliefs.

I was very aware that the information Shaun was giving me didn't fit with any of my own beliefs. Why would anyone have a life purpose of taking their own life? On a personal level I couldn't accept what he was asking me to convey.

I could feel the colour rising in my cheeks but I couldn't pass on to Mum and Dad something I didn't believe, something I didn't think was 'right'.

My thoughts were racing, triggering a raft of uncomfortable emotions. When people come to see me it is usually because one of their loved ones has died and they are feeling the pain of losing them out of their physical lives. They come to me because they hope I can show them that their loved ones are okay even though they no longer have a physical form. My role is to provide survival evidence to show that their loved one lives on, and in doing so bring comfort and closure.

If I passed on what Shaun was telling me it might only bring more distress to his parents. If I was having trouble accepting what Shaun was telling me, his mum and dad might too, and it might bring the whole communication into doubt. It was better to hold back this strange piece of information until I was sure that was what he meant.

Internally, I was frantically seeking more information from Shaun. I didn't want to lose my link with him and was very aware that if I didn't pass on what he wanted his spirit could just withdraw from me through frustration.

Shaun was silent for a while and I found myself being reminded of a young man I had met years ago who had also been suicidal. In all other areas of his life this other young man had been fine. He had a beautiful girlfriend who loved him dearly, a good job, no financial worries and yet when we talked he always said he had a really strong feeling within him that he wasn't to stay here long and that he was to take his own life. He had talked about his childhood at length and said it had been 'idyllic'. He just felt that he was supposed to take his own life.

Over the years many counsellors had worked with him and still the feeling remained. I checked on more than one occasion that he didn't have a negative entity with him urging him to end his own life, and to the best of my knowledge and experience he didn't. It was odd that no one who knew him was really surprised when he eventually fulfilled his prophecy and ended his own life.

At the time his relationship was going through a sticky patch but everyone knew that that was only the trigger, not the cause. He had been planning how he would go for many years. He couldn't ever see or imagine himself as an older person.

I knew that my being reminded of this other young man was no coincidence. He too had felt that taking his life was his life purpose — that it was what he was here to do. The first young man's view I had been able to dismiss until now, but I had just come across a second young man who shared the same viewpoint. It opened up within me a possibility I had not considered before — that there may be people here who, come what may, end up taking their own lives because at some level it is what their soul or their personality self has chosen to experience.

'Soul' is that individuated aspect of consciousness that lives and experiences through our physical form. Our 'personality' is the person we think we are. On a personality level we may think that we need to fix certain things about us or our lives, but on a soul level these matters may not be of concern to us. Soul is primarily concerned with the expression of soul qualities: love, compassion and a return to known oneness with everything/God.

What to do? What should I say? My logic and reason did not like this different viewpoint one little bit, because it conflicted too strongly with my own belief that it is wrong to take your own life. I believed, and still do, that all life is sacred and to be valued. It was an area I would have to explore in more depth later so that I could resolve it within myself, but Shaun's parents were again waiting for me to speak. I had been silent for quite a while now.

Shaun was still adamant he wanted me to tell his parents that it had been what he *had* to do. A bit of me was still questioning, not ready yet to commit to speaking. Perhaps Shaun had an entity with him telling him it was what he had to do? Perhaps in spirit world he was still affected mentally by this spirit? But that honestly didn't feel true. Shaun was spirit world side, energetically clear, happy and at peace. Why would he lie about something like this? It didn't make sense. Still he pressured me to say what he had told me, that he had *had* to take his own life — it was what he came here to do.

Hell, I was in a fix. I take responsibility for what I do very seriously. I didn't want to blurt out what I was being told and cause more pain and I certainly didn't want to get the message wrong — I didn't know if it was my own beliefs that were blocking the communication or just my internal sense of it not being appropriate to pass it on. All I knew was that I didn't want to make this whole situation any more painful than it already was.

Silently I asked Shaun what else he could tell me — perhaps the bigger picture would help me fit what he had said into a broader perspective, one my mind could accept.

Shaun felt guilt and remorse for what he saw his family and friends going through but not an ounce of regret. I passed on the former but not the latter as I was still not ready to go there.

Shaun showed me, using images and feelings, that he had planned his death very carefully. He had made sure this time that Dad, not Mum, had found him.

This time? I questioned. He showed me that there had been a previous attempt and it had been Mum who had found him; it had affected her deeply. This time he was found by Dad.

Shaun talked about the circumstances of his death and slowly, piece by piece, I passed on the information to Mum and Dad, carefully gauging their reactions as I went. It can be very painful hearing about how your loved one died, especially when they have taken their own life. It was clear though that I was not telling them anything they did not already know.

They explained to me that Shaun had gone to extraordinary lengths to make sure that Mum was not the one to find him this time. Mum had phoned him during the day and he had fabricated a story about what he was doing to ensure she stayed out of the house. He had covered up his feelings about what he was about to do very well, and she hadn't suspected a thing.

I knew that as painful as the circumstances of his death had been for his parents to hear, they had needed to hear them. I could not know the details of how he died, and so it confirmed for them that I really did have Shaun with me and that he truly was all right.

Inside Shaun was still badgering me to tell Mum and Dad the rest.

'Tell them,' he insisted. 'Tell them the rest.'

The room was silent and it was clear to Mum and Dad that I still had Shaun with me and yet wasn't speaking. They were watchful, waiting for me to speak again. My resistance to Shaun's persistence was wearing thin. I found myself suspending reason and logic and telling his parents exactly what he wanted me to.

'Look, I have only ever seen this twice in twelve years,' I said, explaining myself before Shaun's words were even out of my mouth. 'He is telling me that he fully intended to take his own life. That it was what he *had* to do this lifetime.'

I quickly went on to talk about the other young

man I had known who had held this view and who had also taken his own life. Before I could speak further, Mum interrupted.

'It's all right, we know,' she said quietly.

It was as though I hadn't heard her. I kept on elaborating. Shaun's explanation poured through me.

'He was going to do it at some time. It was just a matter of when. You couldn't watch him all the time. It was what he *had* to do. He was going to do it somehow.'

My head was a jumble. How could he have *had* to take his own life? Then I found myself recalling what Mum had just said: 'It's all right, we know.' Time to shut up, I told myself, and to listen — this time to Mum.

Mum explained that this had been exactly how Shaun had talked. That to him it seemed it would only be a matter of time before he did take his own life. That it was what he was supposed to do. That as odd as it all seemed, this had been their view as parents too: that they were not going to have him in their lives forever, that one day he would take his own life.

This precious piece of information that I was desperately trying to withhold was the one thing that they were actually waiting for me to say. I had their Shaun and he was okay, he was where he wanted to be. Mum was smiling now for the first time. She *knew* I had her boy.

I found myself wondering. Had he been mentally ill? He certainly didn't feel like he was mentally ill in spirit world — he was peaceful and happy. Shaun showed me a drug, one he had taken some time previously, perhaps two or three years before. The drug had somehow caused him to disconnect internally from his feelings and from his true self. Living like that had been dreadful for him. It had been like being dead inside, no matter what he did.

Since that time it would have been difficult for anyone to have connected with him, even Mum and Dad. When we disconnect internally, on a physical level we also disconnect from those we love, we disconnect from life and from the earth. The physical experience is merely a reflection of what is happening internally.

Shaun hadn't tried to mend the internal connection because connecting with life and his loved ones would have held him here longer and he didn't want to be here any more.

Now he was spirit-world side he was connected with all life again — and with Mum and Dad. He felt good again — whole. It was better than he ever imagined.

Before the communication ended Shaun showed me a letter he had left behind, smiled, and nodded at me to ask Mum about it.

'Shaun's telling me about the letter, his letter. He wants me to ask you about the letter,' I said. There were tears rolling down Mum's cheeks.

'It was a beautiful letter, full of love and compassion,' she said.

It wasn't a hurtful, sad or angry letter like people who take their own lives usually leave, it was a beautiful letter explaining what I was now telling them but in much better words.

It was only after Shaun's mum and dad had left that I was at last able to reflect on what this communication really meant. Was it possible that a soul would incarnate here knowing that it would at some stage choose to end its physical life?

Now I was alone I could ask my guides about the truth of this concept. I didn't waste any time as my mind was really struggling with this one.

The response I received took me by surprise. Instead of affirming or denying the situation a whole new concept was given. One I wasn't really ready for at the time.

Everyone chooses when and how they die. Some choices are made consciously as Shaun's was and others are made unconsciously. Visually I was shown a person choosing to work with hazardous chemicals spraying crops, another choosing to drive when they were tired and yet another smoking. We all suicide sooner or later, it's just that some of us take longer to die. If we are not nurturing ourselves (making life-affirming choices) we are killing ourselves.

It wasn't the answer I expected. I was still feeling my reaction to it when more information followed.

If you accept that you are eternal and that part of you lives forever, experiencing, growing and learning, isn't it possible that somewhere along that path one of the choices might be suicide, for whatever reason? You may choose suicide because you see it as the only solution to the pain, be it mental, physical or emotional. You may choose suicide because you see it as a way of facing your fear of death. You may see suicide as the honourable thing to do, as in the Japanese samurai culture, or choose it for many different reasons.

It is a choice. Sometimes the choice is well thought through and sometimes it isn't. It is still a choice, and all our choices have consequences. As we experience the consequences of our choices we learn more about ourselves and about this reality, and then we make another choice and see how that feels too. We learn through our experiences what are life-affirming choices for us and what aren't, and over time we get to make better choices, for ourselves and for those we love.

THE SNOWDROP

A snowdrop doesn't worry if something's right or wrong,
A snowdrop doesn't worry if it doesn't yet belong
To a group of people or to a certain place,
A snowdrop has no worries about religion, creed or race.
A snowdrop does the thing it knows just how to do,
It shoots up in the springtime to tell us winter's through,
In the early sunshine while other flowers hide,
The snowdrop's driven to appear by feelings deep inside.
The first of all the flowers to dare to show its face,
Connected with all nature, the snowdrop knows its place,
A beautiful reminder on a cold and frosty day,
To be myself no matter what and then I'll find my way.

9. Forgiveness

Jacqui was brought to see me by her mother. Mum hadn't gone into details with me when she phoned, but I knew her daughter had been through a rough time and needed some help. I picked up that there had been early childhood trauma, mental and emotional abuse, and possibly sexual abuse. The latter wasn't an area that I was familiar with but, when Mum explained that she didn't know where else to turn, I agreed that I would see her daughter when I was next in town. We booked a healing appointment for the following Saturday.

Mum drove Jacqui to the appointment. Jacqui was just eighteen but looked much older because of the weight she was carrying. Mum made her excuses and left. I wasn't sure if it was because she wanted Jacqui to be able to speak freely to me or because she herself couldn't handle Jacqui talking about what had happened. I suspect it was a combination of both. It didn't matter because it was better that Jacqui and I were alone.

I have been fortunate this lifetime not to have experienced physical, mental, emotional or sexual abuse as a child. I know that many here have not been so lucky. In some families there have been horrific levels of abuse that have effectively been condoned by other family members who do nothing and say nothing, and this has made it very hard for those being abused to speak out.

Of all the things I have come across this lifetime the sexual abuse of children is the hardest thing for me to forgive. When people like Jacqui started crossing my path, coming for healing, attending workshops and talking to me at the mediumship shows, I knew that the universe was trying to draw my attention to my feelings about child abuse. For some reason the universe was wanting me to understand sexual abuse better.

I don't know what it is like, but I have spent a lot of time sitting with and listening to people who have been abused. Men as well as women. It doesn't get any easier to hear their stories and it makes no difference if the person talking is sixteen or sixty: the pain of the stories, emotionally, mentally and physically, is still evident. Every story, every experience is unique. Jacqui's story began when she was just five years old.

I was surprised at how little time it took Jacqui to open up. I was something of a stranger to her but sometimes complete strangers can be easier to talk to than our nearest and dearest. We can find ourselves recounting a situation to a stranger very differently from the way we recount the same situation to someone close and that is because those close to us expect us to behave a certain way — the same way that we always do with them. With a stranger we may find it easier to speak from the heart and this is why I think anonymous telephone counselling services can be so useful. We hear ourselves talking about a familiar situation in a different way and the listener can help us to put it all into a different and more healthy perspective.

As Jacqui spoke I was aware of many heightened and sometimes conflicting emotions within her: her love for her family, her anger at her uncle and at Mum for knowing what was happening and not stopping it. It was bad enough to have suffered sexual abuse by someone who was supposed to love her, but not being protected by her mother made it a thousand times worse in her eyes. Jacqui grieved for her loss of innocence and feared for her future relationships. She felt dirty and unworthy. She despaired about her weight and at times she wanted to die.

I will spare you the traumatic details, but basically Jacqui was abused by her uncle for six years until her eleventh birthday, when she was at last able to tell a teacher at school. She did it on her birthday as she thought people would be less likely to be mad at her on her birthday. It took a hell of a lot of courage and was a birthday she will probably never forget. Dad, who no longer lived with the family, and was not normally a violent man, had wanted to kill the uncle, Mum's brother. Dad had stormed round to the house and, had the uncle been there, might well have ended up in jail on a murder charge.

There was no communication with the uncle now. Nothing. Auntie for some reason was standing by her man and so the family had lost Auntie out of their lives too. Mum had been heavily in denial when Jacqui first told her what was going on. She had ignored Jacqui's cry for help, and so Jacqui had eventually turned to her form teacher at school.

Jacqui felt responsible for splitting the family up and so on top of all the mental, physical and emotional harm there was this extra level of guilt. Uncle had not gone to jail for what he did. What if he abused another child? Jacqui had her suspicions that he could be abusing her cousin, his daughter, but could not prove anything. Should Jacqui go to the police and then court — and if she did, how would the wider family feel towards her? Would that be vindictive or the right thing to do? I could see there was a lot resting on this young girl's shoulders.

So where to start? I could see that as Jacqui

told me about what had happened to her, she was re-experiencing her feelings from the time. Sometimes I worry that when we simply replay events in our heads we cause ourselves to experience the emotional consequences of those images, and that this doesn't necessarily help. People can go to counsellors for years telling the story again and again and not seem to move forward. How could I best help this young girl to move forward from where she was?

I recognised that the part of Jacqui that was telling the story was her victim part. It was the part of her consciousness that told the story of all she had been through. The victim's job is to tell the story. That is what it does. It loves to tell the story and will tell the story to as many people as will listen, and as many times as people will listen. We all have a victim part, though sometimes we may try to suppress it. The victim's job is to be victimised and to feel sorry for self. In doing so it is trying to get help or attention for self. That is its positive intent. So the victim part telling the story really wanted to get help for Jacqui and that was a good sign.

Jacqui was a tangled mess of emotions and thoughts. She just didn't know where to file some of the things she had experienced and felt. It looked as though the whole situation was in danger of overwhelming her. I could see that she badly needed a different way of seeing this, one that would help her heal and grow.

My guides worked with me to take Jacqui through a process. I started by getting her to lie down on the healing table. Lying down helps us to relax more deeply than sitting and it also conveys a message; we have been sitting talking about this situation and now we are going to do something different.

As Jacqui settled herself I asked her to close her eyes and focus on her breathing. When we close our eyes we shut out all the visual distractions, and when we focus on our breath our attention goes out of the mind and we find ourselves starting to relax. The breath is the interface between the physical and the spiritual. It is what keeps our spirit self in this physical form. Focusing on the breath is very good for quietening us internally and Jacqui's turbulent emotions could certainly do with calming.

'Imagine yourself as a young child,' I said quietly.

'How young?' came her response.

'No particular age, just let your awareness see yourself as a younger age and then let me know when you can see yourself. Maybe you will see a photo of yourself at a particular age, and that is okay too.'

It took a few moments before Jacqui could see her inner child.

'I can see myself,' she said eventually.

'Good. What age do you look as though you are?'

'Eleven. It is my eleventh birthday.'

'How do you look as though you are feeling?' I asked tentatively.

'Afraid,' Jacqui's face had changed and her voice was quieter now.

'Are you happy to go across to yourself as the grown-up you and say "Hello" to this eleven-year-old young girl?'

'Okay,' said Jacqui apprehensively.

'So do that now and let me know what happens,' I instructed. I could see Jacqui's face grimacing as the grown-up her went over to talk to the eleven-year-old inner child. She was silent for a little while so I had to prompt her to tell me what she was experiencing.

'What's happening?' I inquired.

'Nothing. She just turned her back.'

'Can you still see her?' I asked.

'Yes,' Jacqui said, 'but she is facing away from me like she doesn't want to see me or talk to me.'

'Let her know that you have come to help,' I said reassuringly.

Jacqui frowned momentarily. 'She is shaking her head. She doesn't trust me.'

'Let her know that you are the grown-up her and you have come to help,' I gently prompted.

'She is angry at me. She wants to know where I was.'

I could see that this exchange was a very real experience for Jacqui and that was a good sign.

'Tell her you are sorry that you couldn't be there for her before but that you are here for her now.'

There was a silence once more.

'What's happening?' I gently prompted.

'She has turned around to face me again.'

'Is she looking at you?'

'No, she is looking at the floor.'

'Okay,' I said. 'Reach out your hand to her. Let her know you are very sorry for what has happened to her. You are with her now, you are the grown-up her and you will ensure that this never happens again.'

It took a while but gradually Jacqui's face brightened.

'She is looking at me now,' she said.

'That's good. You are doing really well. Let her know that we can't change what has happened but that you can help her look after herself from this point on.'

As soon as Jacqui had done this I explained that when we talk to our inner child it is very important that we do not lie or promise anything we cannot deliver. Communication has to be truthful. The grown-up Jacqui could assure the inner child that the child abuse would not happen again, but could not, for example, make everything all right.

'How is she feeling now?' I asked when Jacqui had had a little time with her inner child.

'I don't know,' said Jacqui.

'Ask her,' I gently prompted. 'Ask her how she

is feeling.'

'Better, but still very angry.'

'Angry about what and towards whom?' I asked.

'Angry at herself for not speaking up sooner, angry at Uncle for doing what he did and lying to everyone. Angry at Mum for not protecting her.'

It was time to reassure the inner child that all these feelings were valid.

'Let her know it is okay to be angry, that all of her feelings are justified,' I assured her.

'Now she is angry at herself for getting angry,' Jacqui said.

'And that's okay too,' I affirmed. 'Ask her — would she like a hug?'

'Not yet, thank you. She's still very angry . . . and hurt.'

'Hurt?'

'Hurt that Uncle, who was supposed to love her, and who told her he loved her, could do this to her and put her in this awful situation.'

'Let her know you understand how she feels — you feel the same way.'

'She's hurt that Mum didn't notice something was wrong,' Jacqui said.

'That's understandable too.'

'Now she is crying.'

'Good. Let her cry and when she is ready, give her a hug if she will let you, or hold her hand.'

There was a longer silence this time but I knew

the tears were healing the past hurt. I sent Jacqui and her inner child love and healing energy as they cried silently together.

'She let me hug her,' Jacqui said, when she was ready to speak again.

'That really is wonderful,' I said. It was. Jacqui had taken a huge step forward.

'How is she feeling now?' I asked when Jacqui had had time to wipe her eyes.

'Much better.'

I needed to understand whereabouts in the feeling range the inner child was now. Much better could still mean pretty dreadful but better than before.

'On a scale of one to ten, if ten is happy, how happy is she?' I asked curiously.

'About a five,' came the reply.

I saw that we still had a way to go. And there was only one person who could let me know how we would get there: Jacqui's inner child.

'What needs to happen before she can feel like a ten?' I asked.

'She needs to know what to do about Uncle, whether she should go to the police.'

'Now that is a hard one for an adult, let alone an eleven-year-old. How about she lets the grown-up her, you, make that decision, with her help of course. Are you, the grown-up, happy to take this on?'

'Absolutely. It should be my decision,' said Jacqui.

'Then let her know that. She can hand that one over to you and the grown-up you will decide after talking to her and getting her point of view.'

Jacqui told this to the eleven-year-old within and came back that now she was feeling like a seven out of ten in terms of happiness.

'What else does she want to tell you?' I whispered.

'She is just saying thank you,' Jacqui said.

'I think we have probably done enough for one day,' I said to Jacqui. 'Thank her for all her help.'

Jacqui did. Before we ended the communication I had a suggestion to make to the grown-up Jacqui.

'So that you can find her easily again it is a good idea to place her in your heart centre in the middle of your chest, surrounding her with soft green light for healing and pink light for unconditional love. How would you feel about doing that?' I asked.

'Great,' said Jacqui. 'I would like to talk with her again.'

So I guided Jacqui in how to do this. 'Ask her if she would like to stay in your heart centre.'

'Yes, she would,' Jacqui confirmed.

The grown-up Jacqui invited the eleven-year-old Jacqui into her heart centre so that the next time the grown-up Jacqui wanted to talk with her inner child she would know just where to find her.

Mum couldn't believe the change in her daughter when she returned. The session had taken just under an hour but the progress had been remarkable.

There was still, however, a long way to go. I worked with Jacqui two more times, checking that the eleven-year-old was still okay — and then worked with Jacqui's ten-year-old, eight-year-old and finally five-year-old inner child.

Very often with inner-child work you find that you work backwards through the ages, getting younger as you go. Sometimes you jump about, as the inner child that appears is the one most relevant to what the grown-up person is experiencing in their life at the time of the session.

At each stage the grown-up Jacqui had to meet and introduce herself to the inner child and then get her talking. Sometimes this is easy to do and other times it is more difficult. When the child doesn't want to talk, you have to let the grown-up person spend time just being with their inner child to start building the relationship. When this happens it is a sure sign that the needs and feelings of the inner child have been ignored, denied or suppressed. I have found that it is particularly important to persist with the inner child work as such times.

By the end of three sessions I was happy that Jacqui understood enough of the inner-child process to work with it by herself between our weekly sessions. It was at her third session that she asked: 'What is it you do while I am talking to my inner child that causes me to feel so much better?'

'I don't do anything,' I said. 'You do.'

Jacqui looked perplexed.

'When you see your thoughts and your feelings as a third party, as the grown-up, you are witnessing the inner child's fears and pains, but you are not in there feeling them as you were the first day we met. Rather you are an observer of them. The inner-child process allows you to see your thoughts and feelings for what they are so that you can understand how they arose. When you accept that the feelings were perfectly acceptable for that child back then, the grown-up you no longer resists them. Instead you feel them fully and let them go.

'When we first met, all your unpleasant thoughts and feelings were arising within you, and part of you didn't want to feel these feelings. You did not want to feel the anger, hurt, despair and pain within you, so all those feelings got stuck inside you.

'Any feeling that has not been fully felt or understood remains in your energetic space until you are ready to feel it fully. When you feel it fully it no longer holds you back.

'Have you noticed if you have lost any weight since we started doing this work?' I asked.

'Yes, I think I have,' she said, looking perplexed. 'My clothes have definitely been getting looser but I don't weigh myself any more because it only depresses me.'

'As you let go of the old blocked energy it causes a shift within you and you will find your weight starting to fall off. When we carry excess weight it is like we are waiting (weighting) for something to happen in our lives. In your case you were waiting to let go of all the blocked emotion. You have taken charge of that now and are no longer waiting for it to happen.'

'I thought my weight was more to do with me needing to protect me?' Jacqui questioned.

'It is the same thing on a different level,' I explained. 'On a physical level you needed to be kept safe from your uncle and on an emotional level you were hurt and scared of feeling your feelings. The blocked energy within you caused the weight to be held on the physical level. As you feel the feelings, so the need to hold on to your protection against the outside world diminishes too.'

I could see that Jacqui was happy with this response. She beamed back at me. Her excess weight wasn't going to be so hard to let go of after all.

'So where do I go from here?' Jacqui asked. I could see that she was quite apprehensive about continuing the inner-child work on her own.

'Sit down a couple of times a week and talk with your inner child. As you sit, whichever child you most need to listen to will come forward. Look at how they are feeling and then let the grown-up you go over and ask them how they are feeling. As they talk you listen. Your inner child will guide you. If you get stuck with anything give me a call.'

It seemed that in the next few days, everywhere I turned I was hearing stories of sexual abuse. A good friend confided details of her abuse by two of her brothers, people at the shows spoke of their child abuse, and to top it all the universe brought me a child abuser for healing.

He was a male healing client who disclosed that his poor health was partly due to the stress of a pending court case. He made no secret of the fact he was being prosecuted by the police for the sexual abuse of a number of his own grandchildren. The charges were being brought by his children and his grandchildren.

I didn't understand what it was the universe was trying to teach me. It had been hard listening to Jacqui's story and to my friend's, but now it was even harder listening to the possible child molester who was terminally ill. How was I supposed to find compassion for him?

It really was time for me to look at the bigger picture of what was happening. Why was the universe suddenly bringing into my awareness so many people who had suffered and maybe even been responsible for child abuse? Why bring me a possible child molester for healing?

I knew I was very judgmental of the perpetrators of child sexual abuse. I have seen the damage it does, so I consider it possibly the hardest thing to forgive. It takes things from a person that can take years to recover: their sense of worth, their innocence (innersense).

If the universe was expecting me to forgive my client it would have to help me. I did the only thing that I could at the time. I handed the whole lot over to God/the universe. I asked to understand child abuse more fully. What was this whole situation showing me? The insights, when they came, came in two parts: the first was about creating our own reality, about changing our thoughts and beliefs, and the second was about forgiveness. When a child is abused, in whatever way, be it physically, emotionally, mentally or sexually, because the child is naturally caring and loving they can't imagine that someone they love could be so 'wrong'. The only conclusion they can reach when someone they love does something bad to them is that it must be *their* fault. It must be the 'badness' inside them that caused this horrible thing to happen. The loss of innocence (innersense) inhibits their natural openness and causes them to lose their internal connection. It can cause a very deep wound, one which may take years to heal. But it *can* be healed as the 'victim' starts to understand what really happened and learns to love and trust themselves once more.

I was reminded of how we create our own reality. When we experience something we view that experience in a particular way. Experiences that feel bad we label as 'bad' and then seek to avoid, and experiences that make us feel good we label as 'good' and want more of. With sexual abuse the child will label the experience as 'bad', as something they want to avoid, but because they experience it as such a bad thing there is a strong emotional attachment to it — they *really* do not want it to happen again. They start fearing it happening again.

The universe is impartial. It is made of energy as we are made of energy. It is a universal law that like attracts like, energetically speaking. The danger is that if you feel bad inside because of what has happened to you, and you fear it happening again, you are putting out a powerful combination of negative energy that is likely to create more negative experiences. These negative experiences then further reinforce that the 'victim' is a 'bad' person and that 'bad' things happen to them. It creates the illusion of powerlessness.

To break the cycle we have to become conscious of what is *really* happening. Once the 'victim' can see and understand that it is *how they are thinking and vibrating* that is attracting further negative experiences, they are highly motivated to change their thoughts and feelings so that they can draw more positive experiences to themselves.

Rarely do any of us actually experience what is. Instead we are constantly experiencing people, events and situations through our own particular blend of filters and beliefs. Life does not just happen to any of us. We create it moment by moment through our thoughts and feelings. The 'you' that is reading this is the product of all the thoughts and feelings you have had up to this point in time, and your future experiences are determined by the thoughts and feelings you choose to think and feel now.

Jacqui was learning that she could change the feelings and beliefs within her. She was no longer choosing to live her life though the eyes of her victim part. The victim part of us perceives that the past is more powerful than the present, and when we stand back from this perception we can see that this is not an empowered way to see our life.

In contrast, an empowered person realises that it is how they are in this moment that creates their future. If Jacqui chose not to let her past experiences affect who she was, not through denial or blocking them but through bringing them into her conscious awareness and seeing them for what they were, she could create an altogether better and more loving future for herself.

The second part of the insight focused more on forgiveness.

Everything that happens to us in life is a mirror. Every person, situation or event.

When we ask 'What is this mirroring in me?' meaning 'What belief or thought am I holding that this situation is mirroring?', we are taking responsibility for what is happening in our lives. We are not judging what happens as good or bad, instead we are looking at the situation as the creator not as the victim.

We are also accepting what is. *Acceptance is a higher vibration than forgiveness as it contains no judgment*. Forgiveness implies that there has been a wrongdoing. It can keep us in victim mode; someone has done something to us and they need to apologise.

As creators of our reality we know that only we create our experience of reality; no one else does. We are responsible for everything that happens to us, and by knowing this we are empowered to know that we can create something else for ourselves if we so wish.

Acceptance says that all is as it should be — that whatever is happening is assisting us to grow. If we view life as perfect, no matter what happens, we are naturally in the energy of *love* and we feel at peace.

Whenever we feel angry, hurt or any other emotion that we consider negative, we hold that energy within us. It isn't because of what someone else did. The situation just reflected what was already within us, the anger or hurt that was already there. Life is a mirror that enables us to see what we are carrying within ourselves on an energetic level so that we can heal, grow and change.

I was curious. What was my part in all of this? Why were so many child abuse issues coming into my life? What was the mirror for me? I understood that I had to explore how I felt about child abuse and then see it from a different, higher, perspective if I was ever going to be able to accept it.

And what was the mirror for Jacqui? That, I would find out at our next meeting.

The session went well and I relayed to her the insights I had received. I gave her some time to think about what the mirrors for her could be.

Jacqui realised that she had felt powerless. That things could happen to her in life and that she was powerless against them. She had felt powerless about her own emotions, powerless to get her mother's attention to what was going on. Powerless to get help.

She also realised that through our session she had recovered her power. She had witnessed her feelings and understood where the feeling of powerlessness came from. She didn't feel powerless any more. She had got her mother's attention, she had got herself help. She had had the courage to feel her emotions.

I noticed that for the first time in three sessions Jacqui hadn't asked me about Uncle and what she should do, so I asked if she had made up her mind.

She nodded. 'I know that he didn't really mean to hurt me, that he does love me. It is just that somehow his thinking has got distorted. I think he needs help more than anything. I have spoken with Mum about getting him some help and about counselling for the whole family. I don't need to punish him. But I do need to know he won't keep doing what he has done to me to others. I think he has a little boy inside of him that is really afraid.' I think she could just be right.

It was amazing to see that Jacqui had been able

to move so far in such a short space of time. Now she was coming from a place of compassion rather than hurt and anger, all of a sudden the way forward was clearer to her. Funny how when we are clearer within, we end up being clearer about what needs to happen without (in our physical lives). So if you are ever not clear about your direction in life, remember it is just a mirror for what is going on inside — and it is time to clear out some of those old beliefs and feelings that no longer serve you.

10. Helping People to Die

Although I am undoubtedly best known for my abilities as a medium, I consider that my higher ability is as a healer. In fact when my first guide appeared physically to talk to me on the London Underground twelve years ago he told me that I was here as a healer and a teacher — he didn't mention mediumship. I find that rather interesting.

Often we think of the healer's job as helping people to get well and that certainly is the main aspect but there is also another more difficult aspect — helping people to die.

Rose was a client who, during a private consultation, asked me for an opinion of her husband's health. Her husband Ralph, who was in his mid-sixties, was not with us at the time and as I tuned in to his name and age I sensed that he had that English reserve that is so common in men of his generation.

'Yes, he is English,' she said, 'and very much as you describe.'

I felt concern — his and hers — there was a matter that needed tests doing but I could sense Ralph was scared both of having the tests and of receiving the results. He had been covering things up for a while, not wanting to worry Rose.

I conveyed what I had received as best I could and then Rose explained that Ralph had been having trouble with his waterworks for years and had now developed a very noticeable growth in the prostate area. She was very worried about it.

Ralph, like many men of his generation, was uncomfortable talking to doctors about matters of a more personal nature and so when he had trouble 'down below', as he described it, he didn't go to see his doctor. But the symptoms were clearly getting worse.

Rose could see the swelling and when she came to see me she thought that the growth might weigh as much as a kilo. It was really noticeable and she was at her wits' end because Ralph would not go and see his doctor.

Strange as it seems, a growth of this size in the prostrate area can still be benign, but my feeling was that she must make an appointment for him. It did not feel good to me. If there was a problem it could be dealt with and sooner rather than later —

and if it was harmless, at least her mind would be at rest. She nodded and agreed that if he wouldn't act she must. She made an appointment for him the next day and tricked him into taking her to the doctor's. It was only when they were in the doctor's room that she came clean.

By the time Ralph was examined by his doctor and then by a specialist it was very clear that Ralph had aggressive prostate cancer that had already spread to other parts of his body. Prostate cancer is cancer of the small, walnut-shaped gland in men that produces seminal fluid, the fluid that nourishes and transports sperm.

For many men a diagnosis of prostate cancer can be very frightening, not only because of the threat to their lives, but also because of the threat to their sexuality. Ralph had been understandably frightened and his fear had kept him from thinking clearly. If prostate cancer is detected early — when it's still confined to the prostate gland — there is a better chance of successful treatment. Once the cancer has spread beyond the prostate gland successful treatment can be more difficult.

I didn't hear any more for several months until Rose again sought my help, this time as a healer. The doctors had advised Ralph that there was nothing left they could do. Like many natural healers, I find that many of those who come to see me are seeing me as a last resort. They have tried conventional forms of treatment and then when the doctors cannot offer anything else, they come to see me. How I wish that many of them would come to me sooner than they do, then they would have a much better chance of recovery.

Although people commonly refer to me as a healer, I consider the term 'healer' something of a misnomer. I do not actually heal anyone; the patient heals themselves using energies that are channelled through me.

When I first started working with people with terminal illnesses I felt tremendous pressure to make them well. The patient and their family are hoping against hope that they will beat the condition, and they can place unwarranted faith in you simply because they do not want to face the prospect of death. As a healer you soon come to understand that it is not healthy nor desirable for your ego to be engaged in the healing process. Some people receive miraculous healings and some people don't. Some get better enough to work out what they are doing or thinking to cause the condition and then they can release it. Others don't.

Every condition is different and every healing is different. I have seen people with liver cancer live, and others with less serious complaints die. You have to face each patient and each healing session with a completely open mind. Very often when people are facing a terminal illness they have had surgery, chemotherapy or radiation treatment. Many are tired of trying and tired of life because it lacks the quality it used to have before they got sick.

Sometimes the healing is simply a case of stretching out my hands and allowing the energies through. Other times I have to help the patient to see how and why they have manifested their condition. For some, that alone is a hard ask. Many cannot really accept that they have chosen cancer, or whatever their condition is, for themselves.

I know it can be a difficult concept to grasp that we have ourselves created the condition within us — I mean why would anyone choose cancer? But somehow, through our thoughts, beliefs and feelings, we have. Nothing can happen in this dimension without a cause. The condition is only a result — we have to find the underlying cause. It can be physical cause, if we have, say, been in contact with toxic chemicals and this has damaged our body, but more commonly it will have a mental/emotional cause or link.

Part of the healer's job is to help the patient see what they cannot: how they have created the condition within them. The patient has enough on their plate sometimes and so at some sessions you may just do a straightforward healing. This was the case with Ralph. It was his family who had suggested that he come for healing, and for the first few sessions we made small talk and I gave him healing.

When I give a healing I start by clearing my own

energetic space so that nothing I have been thinking or feeling will negatively affect the patient. Then I ask that my healing guides and the patient's healing guides be present. Then I ask for the healing from a higher power. The words I use, and that I have used for many years now, are:

'Mother, Father, God, I ask you for the healing of this your own child and I thank you. Amen, Amen, Amen.'

I am very comfortable with this particular wording as it encompasses most people's beliefs. I then allow myself to be entirely guided by the guides that are present and by the consciousness of the energy. My hands move sometimes very intricately and sometimes very forcibly. I can experience heat, cold, tingling, prickling and a number of other sensations. I can feel energy blocks being cleared and crystalline structures being removed. Sometimes it feels like I am doing surgery within the body. An average session takes something like twenty minutes but sometimes they are just three or four minutes, particularly when I am doing public demonstrations. At the end of the session I am shown that the healing is complete.

Sometimes during a session I will intuit what else a person needs to do to facilitate their healing. I may advise on diet, recommend a particular book that the person will find useful, or recommend another kind of complementary treatment that will be beneficial for the patient.

After just a couple of weeks, Ralph reported that his sessions with me seemed to be helping. The swelling was feeling less uncomfortable and he was sleeping better. As his confidence in me and in the healing grew, I could also see that he was starting to feel more at ease with me. We started to talk about his life and his feelings. I suspected he had not even talked with his family about some of the things he said. Over time I was able to start introducing him to the concept that the mind, body and spirit are connected and then together we started exploring his different beliefs and thoughts, looking for anything that would give a clue as to why this condition had been created in his physical body.

It can take time to do this kind of work and sometimes when people come to see me it just isn't available; their disease is too far advanced, or they are too tired to do the inner work required. In those cases I do the healing and the patient then uses the healing energy in the best way they can. Sometimes it is to pass out of their physical form and into the spiritual dimensions. The patient's higher self always knows best.

If you look at the word disease you will see that it can be broken down into dis-ease, meaning not at ease. Whenever we are not at ease in our lives for any length of time dis-ease will manifest in our physical form. The body stores that dis-ease as blocked energy in a place relative to the kind of dis-ease it is. For example, if we are pissed off about something, the blocked energy or the dis-ease is likely to be in the bladder. If we are having problems with our legs, which support our body, then we need to explore how we are not feeling supported. All ill-health conditions are indicators that we are not at ease or are resisting something. If we can recognise what it is we are resisting, then simply by bringing that knowledge into the light of our consciousness, we can start releasing the tension (blocked energy) in that part of the body. As the energies unblock, the body naturally starts to heal itself. The body has remarkable healing abilities if we get out of its way and allow it to heal itself.

In Ralph's case the healing came too late to keep him alive as the damage to his physical form was already very advanced, but it did help him understand himself better and pass peacefully when the time came, and I knew that to him and his family that meant a lot.

I have met many people, women as well as men, who have been very sick but have tried to hide it from their loved ones and refused to see a doctor. Sticking our heads in the sand when we know there is something wrong with our bodies is not a life-affirming choice. As a strategy it sucks! We owe ourselves and our families something better.

As human beings, while we have a physical body, illness and death are a part of our life and all of us will have to face them at some time. Dealing with our health issues responsibly and effectively can help give meaning to our lives if we let it. In finding the correct solutions and remedies to the energy blocks within us we develop knowledge of ourselves and can thus enrich our lives, as Ralph did. It is sad that he found this out as late as he did, because his life had the potential to be much more rewarding than it was.

When we don't take responsibility for our health it can often add to the suffering of those left behind. Ralph was in a better place himself but the family he left behind, as well as feeling the pain of losing him out of their physical lives, were also trying to come to terms with his behaviour. If only he told them what he was experiencing. If only he had gone to the doctors to get himself checked out. A burning question inevitably remained: if he had sought medical intervention and healing earlier would he still be alive? I suspect he would.

So what can we learn from stories like Ralph's? We know that we exist in a physical body and we can see that at some stage in our lives there will most likely be some kind of sickness and suffering. If we are able to accept this as part of life we will be able to cope with it better when the time comes, and this applies whether it is our illness or the illness of a loved one.

By thinking about both illness and death before they arise we can train ourselves mentally so that we will be much better able to deal with such problems when they arise. It is our responsibility to look after our bodies. If we look after our health on a day-to-day basis our body will be that much better able to cope with illness when that time comes.

The great Indian scholar Shantideva said: 'If there is a way to overcome suffering, there's no need to worry. If there's no way to overcome suffering, then there's no use in worrying.'

So, when we face health problems and the prospect of death we should look for the solution, seeking help from conventional and complementary health practitioners. We should also look within to see what it is within ourselves that is causing the health problem or threat to our life to manifest.

Our energies are best engaged in looking for a solution rather than worrying. In some cases, when we cannot find a solution, then we have to accept the situation, and there is still no point in worrying. Worrying will aggravate the condition as the resultant tension stresses the physical body still further.

As human beings we seem to have two basic ways of approaching death. The first is to put it completely out of our minds, pretending we are indestructible and that it will never happen to us. The second is to spend time thinking about the nature of death, analysing it as you would any other problem. I have met a great many people who do not like thinking about death because it makes them feel uncomfortable. This way of thinking does not help eliminate or minimise the suffering of death.

Many people dealing with particularly traumatic situations such as the loss of a child did not think it could happen to them or their loved ones. Then when the tragedy hit their child, not only was there the pain of physical separation from their loved one, but there was also a massive shock to their belief system.

The alternative approach is to analyse death before that time draws near. By doing so, you become familiar with it and you come to understand that death *is* a part of our life. It is inevitable and cannot be avoided. In this physical form, sooner or later we all die.

At some stage in our lives, preferably before we are on our death beds or about to lose one of our loved ones, we need to think about impermanence and death.

We are all made of flesh and blood. Our physical bodies are impermanent. Physical death will come sooner or later to each of us, whether it is natural or accidental. If we are able to accept this and prepare for it, it will be much easier to face when the time comes.

I was invited to visit Abigail through a friend of a friend. Abigail had just entered palliative care, and, at thirteen years of age, she was in lots of ways still a child — a very affectionate one.

From our very first meeting it seemed to me that the family were really in anticipatory grief — they were getting ready for the 'beginning of the end' in their minds. I wasn't at all sure how I felt about that. Granted, Abigail was in palliative care but even so, wasn't accepting that she was dying as much playing God as being sure that she would survive?

Wouldn't it be better to accept the symptoms arising in the now and deal with that? Accepting what was — neither resisting nor accepting death — accepting what was, right at that moment?

I could see that the family was already grieving, especially Mum, who was preparing her psyche for the loss of her child.

Often when I have had the opportunity of being with family members in palliative care I have found there have been long silences while sitting with them. The atmosphere has felt relatively comfortable given the circumstances but the exceptionally long silences have at times left me feeling a little awkward. I have learned that often you don't need to say anything, you just need to be there.

Anticipatory grief is generally more silent than grief after a loss; it is not something people talk about. It's a grief that we tend to keep to ourselves. There is little or no need for words, as feelings can be comforted by the touch of a hand or silently sitting together. Sometimes we can underestimate just how much of a comfort this simple act is and I only know this because afterwards people have told me how beneficial it was, just my being there for them. At the time I had worried that I wasn't doing enough or wasn't saying the right thing.

Sitting with Mum silently now I could see her dilemma. She so dearly wanted to be positive but also wanted to be realistic. They had tried many different avenues to try to get help and healing for Abigail. Mum just wanted to know how long the family had left with her. It may seem an odd question to ask. In a way it is, but sometimes if families knew how long they had, better work arrangements could be made. I have only twice had prior knowledge of when someone was going to die. It is a choice that is made by the person day by day, moment by moment, to stay here or move on. I have never asked to be shown when someone will pass away because to me that is almost like playing God, and it wasn't something I was going to ask now. The timing of Abigail's passing would be up to her. If the pain got too extreme for her she might want to die sooner.

'I am sorry,' I answered Mum. 'That isn't something I can tell you. The doctors may have more of an idea.'

Mum nodded. 'They have told us two to three months.'

'The best advice I can give you is to make the most of each day. Enjoy each moment you have with her.'

Usually when we grieve we are focused on the loss that has occurred but with anticipatory grief we are thinking about the loss ahead, trying to somehow prepare ourselves for it. Mum's question to me had confirmed that she was in anticipatory grief.

Perhaps Abigail too was wondering how long she had left. Mum must have read my mind, and her words broke the silence.

'Some days it is as though Abigail is getting ready to leave — I see it in her eyes; she tells me I have to be strong.' Mum was sobbing now. 'It is so hard.'

I nodded and squeezed her hand.

'It is,' I agreed. 'You have been such a good Mum to her,' I said reassuringly.

Mum nodded. She had absolutely done her best and she knew it.

Where there is a long, drawn-out illness and the loved one is preparing for the physical separation from this world, they will often go through the same change or grieving process that we looked at in Chapter Two (see page 42).

The loved ones who remain here go through it too. We may not realise what is happening at the time. We may feel it simply as a strange feeling in the pit of the stomach or an ache in our heart that we feel before our loved one dies. I could sense this sad feeling in Abigail's mum as we sat together. She was holding so much of her emotion in for the sake of her daughter and the wider family.

'You need to take some time off, for you, to feel what you are feeling,' I said.

I knew that Mum was Abigail's primary carer; there were others supporting her but I also knew she was not taking any time out for herself. She didn't like to when the time they had left together was so precious. I could understand that.

'You have to take some time for you — go to the gym, walk in the park, go shopping, anything.' I could see my words weren't getting through. 'If you don't look after you, you won't be able to look after Abigail. You have weeks ahead of you, and you have to look after yourself too.'

I found myself telling the story of a daughter whose mother was terminally ill. The daughter ran her own health down so much looking after Mum that she developed a cold. Mum was nutropenic, with a low white-blood-cell count and a severely compromised immune system, and so the daughter ended up not being allowed in the same room as Mum while she recovered from her cold. This at last seemed to make some impact on her. It was a hard way for me to put the information across but she really did need to take some time out.

It was clear with Abigail's mum that she had already moved beyond denial and blaming. She had nothing but praise for the doctors and therapists who had assisted her daughter on her journey.

'What can I do to help her?' Mum asked, changing the subject.

'Go at her pace. Let her lead the way. Let her know that whatever she is feeling is okay. There will be days she wants to talk and days she doesn't — be flexible to her needs.

'One of the best ways you can help her is to look after you, take some time out for you. She needs to see that you are doing okay. And that you will be okay should she choose to leave.'

I was reminded of an interview I had seen on *Oprah* several years previously. Oprah Winfrey was interviewing a white-haired gentleman with a kindly face. He worked in a hospice with people who were terminally ill.

Oprah was curious and asked, 'What determines how peacefully we die?'

That gentleman put it better than I have ever known anyone express it. He said, 'How peacefully we die is determined by the answers to two questions: how well did we love? and how well were we loved?' I conveyed this to Abigail's mum.

'Abigail is surrounded by so much love it is clear that when her time comes, when she is ready to go, it will be a peaceful passing.' I could tell from Mum's reaction that it was what she had wanted to hear. She needed to know that Abigail would be okay when the time came.

Anticipatory grief can be likened to a river: it has its own process and it takes its own time. However, going through the stages before our loved one dies does not mean that you will not go through these same stages again after the loss. Most likely you will. Forewarned is not always forearmed where grief is concerned. Experiencing anticipatory grief may or may not make the grieving process easier for us — in fact it can bring up feelings of guilt. We can feel guilty that we were grieving before the loss actually occurred. Not everyone experiences anticipatory grief and as always our experience of it is unique to us.

This next story is about a remarkable young woman who faced death bravely when the time came.

Jan and I shared the same birthday and she was perhaps four or five years younger than me. She had two sons a couple of years older than my children. She had booked in with me for a clairvoyant reading but when she arrived she explained that it wasn't what she wanted at all. She just wanted to talk to me about dying.

She looked fine, a little tired maybe but that was all. I wouldn't have suspected anything if I had passed her on the street.

I was puzzled. 'Have you thought about trying healing? That may be able to help you.'

She nodded. 'I think it is too late.'

'Do you mind if I check your energy field and see what is happening?' I offered.

'Sure, if you want.'

I was quite taken aback. There was an energy in her stomach area that I can only describe as ravenous. It was the most aggressive cancer I have ever felt. There was more than one site and I could also feel that there had been radiation treatment — the energetic residue was still discernible.

I knew that even if I did healing on Jan on a daily basis I could not diminish the cancer quicker than it would grow. She was fighting a losing battle.

Jan just looked at me. She had read my face.

'I do know,' she said. 'I know it is my time and I am not afraid to die. I just don't want to leave my boys.'

We sobbed together. It was a long time before we spoke again.

Jan still had tears in her eyes. She knew it was her time and was at peace with this but couldn't bear the thought of how her boys would hurt when she died.

We talked for a long while.

'It is so good to have someone to talk to about this,' she said. 'Everyone in the family expects me to be so positive and I try to be, but on the inside I know that I have done what I came here to do and that it will soon be my time to pass.'

I nodded in understanding.

'I just can't bring myself to tell the boys. They haven't a clue. I keep thinking I will tell them and then I see the adverts on the television describing cancer as a monster and I just can't.'

At the time the Cancer Society was running a series of adverts about the monster cancer.

'They are too young to understand,' Jan continued. 'I know they will be frightened about what this will all mean.'

It was a dreadful situation to be in. Would it be

worse to die unexpectedly and not get the chance to say goodbye to your children? She talked and I listened. She needed someone to listen to her and support her.

The one thing she needed to know more than anything else was: could her negative thinking speed her passing? If she thought she was going to die, which she did, would that accelerate her passing?

'Our thoughts do create our experience of reality,' I said. 'When you say you know that soon it will be your time to pass — is that a thought you have or is it a knowing?'

'A knowing,' she said tearfully, touching her heart.

'You aren't creating this if that is what you mean,' I said. 'It's not your mind thinking all the time about how ill you are — it's the inner "you" that is letting the physical "you" know, so you can do what needs to be done.'

'That's what I feel,' Jan confirmed. 'I just didn't want it to be negative thinking that is causing this.'

'Do you think you think negatively?' I gently enquired.

'No. I am just aware that if I say to my family what I have said to you they will think I am being negative and talking myself into dying.'

'You don't strike me as negative at all,' I said. 'Just realistic . . . and very brave.'

'I feel torn in two at times — I know I will die but

I also know that I don't want to leave my boys.'

Staring death in the face, as Jan was doing, brings everything in your life into very sharp focus. She let go of many of the demands on her time so she could spend more time with her boys. Things that had been important to her suddenly weren't important at all. New priorities surfaced and they were all about people, her connection with her boys and her family. It was all that mattered. She could see that many of the things that had been taking up her time were of no significance, none of it mattered. Had she lived, she told me, her life would have been very different.

By facing death so dramatically she came to understand things about herself that many of us may never grasp.

When I last saw her she told me quietly: 'I know that God is using this experience to bring me home.' She smiled. She had never spoken of God to me before.

Jan died peacefully, as we both knew she would, at her home with her family. The Jan who died was a very different person to the one I had first met a few months before and it was clear that her already good relationships with friends and family had been transformed and were much deeper and more meaningful than ever before.

God uses everything we experience in our lives to bring us home.

11. Something More to Life

One of my great delights in travelling and doing live shows is that I get to meet so many people and hear their inspiring and moving stories of their loved ones who have died.

There have been so many stories that have been recounted to me in person, and through letters and emails. Many occurred for people on the way to one of my shows or on their way home afterwards. It's not that I am doing anything to cause this, it is just that around the time of the show they are perhaps more open to receiving their own messages and so they do.

It seems almost everyone I meet has a story to tell about their own experiences and the evidence they have received that there is something more to life. The stories on these next few pages are among my favourites.

The flying teacup

Debbie came over to talk with me after a show. She was clearly very excited about what had happened during that show. She was very animated as she explained that it had been her nana who had come through in the second part of the show when I was talking to another lady on stage.

For a split second I didn't know what on earth she was talking about. Debbie was convinced that her nana had been at the show with her and a teacup that had whizzed through the air towards me during the show had been her nana's.

I suddenly remembered what she was on about. Earlier that evening during the show, I had been passing on a message to a lady on stage with me when I literally had to duck. A spirit-world teacup with a red rose design came hurtling towards me and I found myself ducking down to avoid being hit, before feeling very silly that I had ducked to avoid something that others couldn't see and couldn't ever have hurt me. It caused some hilarity at the time. The lady on stage with me at the time could not understand the meaning of a flying teacup and so I let it go and continued with the rest of her message from her father who had passed over.

Now here was Debbie saying that the whizzing

teacup was a sign from her late grandmother.

As a medium I am very aware of how much some people want and need messages. It can be easy to make something 'fit' when you really need to know that one of your loved ones is okay. As I looked at the young lady in front of me I explained as kindly as I could that it most probably wasn't her nana.

'Lots of nanas have teacups and a fair few would probably have had red roses on them,' I said, but it was clear that Debbie's belief that it was her grandmother's teacup wasn't going to be dislodged quite so easily.

'I am sure it was hers,' she protested.

'What makes you think it was your nana's teacup?' I asked, baffled at how she could be so insistent.

'The teacup is the only thing of Nana's I have and she always said she would show it to me when she came through.' I nodded. It was plausible, though not very convincing. I hadn't had her on stage with me at the time. Why hadn't Nana taken me to her? Wouldn't she do that first before launching the teacup at me? I have to say I was skeptical of the conclusion Debbie had reached.

'You don't understand,' Debbie said abruptly, thrusting out her handbag for me to see inside. 'I brought Nana's teacup with me to the show. It has sat in my handbag at my feet all night and now look at it,' she said. 'It's broken.' There in her handbag was an identical teacup to the one I had seen being thrown at me. It was in pieces, just as she had said.

I was speechless.

It was her one treasured possession from Nana. I knew that she would not have deliberately broken it. The teacup apparently had served its purpose and given Debbie the proof she needed that Nana was okay and still had the same crazy sense of humour Debbie had loved when she was here. Debbie was delighted it had been broken. I had the distinct feeling she would be treasuring the pieces of the broken cup as a reminder that her nana's spirit was still with her.

For once it was *my* skepticism that had been overcome, rather than the audience's. I had to smile at Nana's originality and I hoped it would not start a trend in spirit world. As a way of getting my attention it was a bit extreme but it goes to show spirits sure can work in unusual ways to provide their evidence and get their messages through.

Alfie's story

Alfie was one of the oldest gentlemen I have ever had at one of my shows. He had come hoping for a message from his beloved wife. After the show he came not to ask for a message but to tell me a story of his own. It is a story that raised the hairs on my arms and is one that I will always remember.

As a young boy of perhaps no more than five or

six years of age, Alfie was very sick. He felt dreadful and just couldn't move. Mum came into his bedroom to bring him a fresh orange juice.

'Here, drink this, Alfie,' she said kindly. 'It will do you good. I have a custard in the oven for you later if you can drink this,' she said and then left the room.

Alfie loved custard, especially when it was made by his mother, but knew there was no way in the world he could ever sit to drink the juice let alone eat the custard. Alfie just lay there, his motionless body propped up on pillows. The next thing he knew he was looking down on the top of his mummy's bed. Mummy was kneeling at the side of her bed, praying. Alfie felt himself up on the ceiling looking down at her.

A man's voice broke the silence, saying, 'Don't worry, Alfie.' It was a kind voice, and with that he found himself suddenly back in his body. Then the man's voice said, 'Now drink your juice,' and Alfie sat up, which moments before had been physically impossible, and drank his juice.

Because of his experience Alfie had always known that there was something else and that had given him great comfort throughout his life, especially when he lost his beloved wife. He shared the story with me in the hope that it might give comfort to someone else.

Losing Daddy

Darryl told me about this vivid memory after one of my shows. At the age of nine she was playing at her friend's house in the garden when the telephone inside the house rang. Normally she and her friends would be so engrossed in their play that they would be oblivious to the ringing of the telephone, but this time was different.

As the phone rang she felt something sink in the pit of her stomach. She had never had a feeling like that before and it completely stopped her in her tracks.

At what seemed like the same time, a voice in her head told her that Daddy had died. She didn't know whose voice it was — it sounded like her own — but she knew instinctively that what she had been told was true. She didn't question it at all. Inside she felt very, very sad and she knew that nothing would ever be the same for her again.

She remembered putting her hands over her ears. She didn't want to hear what her friend's mum was going to tell her, that she had to go home. She ran screaming back into the garden and was still very upset when her grandmother eventually came to collect her.

Darryl was right, life after that was not the same. Life was very different without her dad, but she always knew that there had to be something more, because how did she know just like that? Her father had been a lorry driver and was killed in an accident.

Darryl didn't tell anyone about the voice she heard for a long time. She almost felt guilty about it, as if by knowing about it she had somehow contributed to what happened. Instead she kept it to herself and the knowledge of it got her through some difficult times.

Darryl came to talk to me because she realised that if she had told others sooner it may have helped them — her mum and her younger sister especially. She explained that the experience also caused her to begin her own personal voyage of discovery about the spiritual side of life and as she spoke to me it was clear that she was completely at peace. She knew beyond any doubt that we do live forever.

Grandmother's ring

I love this next story about Grandmother's ring. It's a lovely example of the kinds of things spirits can get up to when they want to give us that extra bit of proof that they are there and watching over us.

I first met Shelley when we were filming my television series, *Dare to Believe*. It was Shelley's grandmother on her mother's side who was intent on getting a message through to her. They had been very close for many years and in lots of ways losing her grandmother had been like losing her own mother. There had been a lot of tears when Grandmother died and Shelley was crying again now as I relayed to her the information Grandmother was giving me. The very last thing Grandmother said was, 'Tell Shelley not to worry about the ring, it will be coming back to her.'

I told Shelley what Grandmother had said and asked her what it meant. Tearfully, Shelley explained that she had been left Grandmother's ring. It was a beautiful ring and she had worn it all the time to help her feel close to her grandmother after she had died. A few weeks previously, while she was feeding the chickens, the ring had flown off her finger. It had been a little loose and she blamed herself for not having it altered. The whole family had joined in the search but no one had been able to find it.

'Do you really think I will get it back?' she asked hopefully. It was what Grandmother had said and I checked with her this was what she meant. Grandmother affirmed it was and explained that it was her way of letting her granddaughter know it was time to let her go. She had been passed over six years and Shelley needed to face up the feelings she had about her grandmother not being with her on a physical level anymore. The loss of the ring brought up all the residual feelings. Once she had let Grandmother go she would get the ring back. That would be her sign that she had let her go. I realised from Shelley's reaction that I would need to explain a little better what Grandmother meant.

'When we let someone go, it isn't that we stop loving them or stop feeling their love for us, it is that we accept they are no longer in a physical body and that they are moving on with their own individual journey. Letting your feelings about losing Grandmother go will enable you to feel your connection with her spirit more, not less. The loss of the ring brought up again the pain of losing her. As you grieve and heal that pain of loss you will actually be able to sense her with you more. You will have let go of your attachment to her being in a physical form.'

Shelley nodded. She said that she had been told before that she had to let Grandmother go but she hadn't really understood what that meant. She had thought that if she let her go she wouldn't sense her again. She was happy now that she knew what she needed to do.

It was about six months later that I received a box of the most wonderful homemade chocolates in the post. In it was a note from Shelley saying that her daughter had just found Grandmother's ring on the mantelpiece in front of a photograph of her grandmother.

It was wonderful news. It meant that Shelley had moved on and that her connection with Grandmother would now be stronger than ever.

It is very common for our loved ones in spirit world to move things around our home: photographs, keys and items that link them with us. Sometimes they will take a piece of jewellery from us, as in Shelley's story, and then return it at a later date. Sometimes we get to know why they took it and others times we don't, we can only speculate.

Still helping

Sometimes the spiritual experiences people have can be really vivid, as they were for Lucy.

When I saw Lucy she was obviously at a very low ebb in her life and possibly suicidal. In the space of three months her close grandfather had died, an uncle had taken his own life and her husband had walked out on her, for another woman, she suspected.

Her grandfather had been coming to her in dreams a lot but she had not experienced her uncle at all and it was his spirit she was most worried about. Lucy had seen her grandfather twice at the end of her bed, and he just smiled. In the dreams he had told her that her husband would be coming back. She didn't want to be kidding herself that he would be coming back when he wouldn't. I guess she was really seeking reassurance from me that she wasn't going mad.

Lucy's grandfather was easy to connect with: a good-natured gentleman in his seventies who explained it was 'early days' yet for Bob, Lucy's uncle, to come through. He was fine but needed to sort himself out still. Yes, it had been Grandfather at the end of the bed. He hadn't meant to startle her; he just knew she needed to know someone was there for her at this time.

The love between Grandfather and Lucy was

lovely to experience. I knew that no matter how down she felt just now she would be all right. She was very well supported by her spirit-world family. I checked with Grandfather about Lucy's interpretation of what he had said to her.

'Did you mean that Dave will be coming back into the marriage?'

'Yes.' Lucy had been right in her perception of the message. There was a further explanation that Lucy needed to understand. 'Dave needs to learn to connect better with Lucy and to communicate better. He has withdrawn from the marriage to sort himself out and determine what it is he really wants.'

Lucy was reassured by this. It was what she wanted to hear but also what she felt in her heart, and she didn't really believe there was anyone else involved.

Grandfather's guidance continued.

'The two of you were brought together by spirit world as you suit each other perfectly. You might not agree with each other on everything' — Lucy smiled — 'but you are still a very good match.'

'I really do believe we should be together!' Lucy exclaimed. 'I just feel he has lost himself at the moment.'

The grandfather explained that Lucy's learning from the experience was to bring into the light of her consciousness her fear of being abandoned. She needed to address this before she and Dave had children together, otherwise she could unconsciously pass this fear onto her children.

The communication with Grandfather really helped put Shelley's mind at rest. She admitted she hadn't told me everything when we first sat down together. Instead, she had held back information to see if I would 'receive' the same guidance. All of the information I gave her matched what she had received from Grandfather. She knew now that she wasn't going mad and that Dave, her husband, would be back.

A near-death experience

It was an uncle of mine who first described to me what a near-death experience is like. My uncle had quite a hard life and uncovered his own natural healing abilities quite late in life. He wasn't one to brag about what he could do, he would just quietly place his hands on the person and the energy would flow. People reported feeling incredible heat.

In lots of ways my uncle was a difficult person for me to get to know. Behind the brash, loud, teasing exterior was someone who had his own spiritual insights and experiences, but he rarely talked about them. I don't know how we got on to the subject but he did tell me that he had a near-death experience not once but twice, and on each occasion he saw an incredible light and was met by an older gentleman who told him it was not his time yet.

My uncle carried this experience with him throughout his life and I know it gave him and my auntie great comfort during the physical trial of prolonged illness he experienced before he died a few years ago.

At the time we talked I knew nothing about the spiritual side of life and to hear my loud and brash uncle talk seriously and sensitively about such a thing made a lasting impression on me. Clearly from the way he talked his experiences had been very real for him.

Since then I have heard many similar stories from adults and occasionally children. In each case there have been similar elements, and an experience in which their life was threatened. They may have been seriously ill, in an accident or under anaesthetic. Each experienced themselves as being separate from their physical body. Each saw a light, which they described as being alive, intelligent and benevolently powerful. Each one experienced overwhelming feelings. Some encountered a deceased person or animal they had loved here, and others experienced a life review in which images of their life here passed before them.

In each case that I have come across, information was also given. In my uncle's case it was to let him know that there was more that he had to do here.

Stop tricking the medium

What fascinates me most about near-death experiences is that each story correlates so well with every other one and that children who have never heard a near-death account in their lives also describe the same phenomenon. This next story is quite a typical one. I got to hear about it partly on stage and partly backstage.

About halfway through one of my shows a lively spirit called Ethel came into me and wanted me to find her daughter. Straight away I felt her energetic link with her daughter in the audience and so went across to her. 'Is your mum called Ethel?' I asked as I approached her.

'Yes,' she responded keenly.

My vision went black, like I couldn't see but I still had my eyes open. 'Two halves' reverberated through me. I was looking for two halves. My whole body had been turned to the left and I was looking along the row of people to my left. I could see again. I was looking for the other half.

And then I saw him — a gentleman sitting seven seats away from her and across an aisle.

'You,' I said, pointing at the gentleman. My eyes were fixed on him.

'You are with her,' I said, pointing back at the first lady. I didn't mean to appear rude, but Ethel was in charge.

'I am her husband,' he admitted sheepishly. The audience laughed.

'Stop tricking the medium and get up on that stage now, the pair of you,' I said quite sternly.

Well, the audience were in stitches. I wasn't

really sure what would happen next but this Ethel seemed like a real character to me. She was talking to these two audience members like they were kids. I wouldn't have dreamed of speaking to anyone like that myself, let alone a couple in their seventies.

When we got on stage I caught the husband nudging the wife.

'I told you she'd come through,' he said. He had known all day his mother-in-law would visit.

They had tried to trick the medium and she and the audience found that really funny.

Ethel lost her 'put on' sternness as we talked on stage. She had been a medium herself and that was why it was so easy for her to communicate with me.

She had known them since they first got together as teenagers and that was why she had spoken to them as she had. She knew that they did not need proof of her presence, they had each been given proof in different ways before. Walter, the husband, nodded that this was very true. Immediately I saw an image of him as a younger man and he was on a roof. Suddenly I was very afraid.

'Why is she showing me that?' I asked, once I had got the fear under control. Walter explained that he had fallen off a roof when younger and had a near-death experience. He saw a dimension where everything was golden, a dimension that many of us would think of as heaven, where everything you want, you get. Then he saw a bright light that felt incredible. The light asked him if he wanted to die. The next moment he was back in his body and made a recovery that completely astounded the doctors. Ethel's daughter and Walter committed to each other as a couple shortly after that.

The golden kingdom Walter described is the one many of us think of as heaven. It is where we go if we have the ability to feel love and express it through kind words and actions. Instead of a blue sky it has a golden one, and a great many spirits inhabit this dimension.

Ethel's communication gave Walter a wonderful opportunity to recount to the audience his near-death experience and I am sure his story touched many that night as Spirit surely intended it to do.

TRUST

I know that you are hurting, I feel your
*   sadness too,*
But when you do not trust me, just what
*   am I to do!*
I keep the world a-turning, your heart
*   a-beating too.*
I guide the seas and oceans and you think
*   I can't guide you.*
The seasons and the weather, they all
*   depend on me.*

My child, you need to look beyond
 the images you see,
To sense the truth in all of this, the wisdom
 from the lie,
To realise beyond all doubt you really
 do not die.
My child, if you are listening you'll find me
 in your heart,
There is no death, for all is change, we
 never are apart.

12. Children and Spirits

One of the questions I am asked most frequently at shows is what people can do if they have a child that they think may be able to see or sense spirit world. In fact, I do not think I have ever done a show where this question has not been asked, either during the questions part of the show, or privately afterwards.

Unfortunately there just isn't the time at the shows to talk about all you can do and so here in these pages I would like to share with you some of the ways that you can help children understand what it is they are experiencing.

The most pressing and very common question I am asked about children is what to do when a child is disturbed by seeing spirits.

Sometimes the child is merely sensing or seeing

one of their own family members who has passed over and generally this does not concern me at all. It is natural for those who have passed over to want to stay in touch with us, and once children understand who is visiting them and that this is natural they react to the experience much more positively.

I get more concerned when I hear stories of children not sleeping at night because they can see and hear things that are frightening them. Sometimes spirits can be attached to a property and so this is the first thing I like to check. Have the problems only occurred since they moved into this particular house? If that is the case the spirits can be helped to move across by your local church.

If the problem is not restricted to one house, for example where a child has similar experiences when they sleep over at other people's houses, it may be that the child is naturally more open than most and will need help closing down before going to sleep. You can teach the child to close down psychically as part of their getting-ready-for-bed routine, and to protect themselves using white light. To do this, all the child or you need do is to intend that their chakras (the wheels that govern their non-physical bodies) are closed to *just the right level for healthy sleep*. Then imagine them in a bubble of white light. It is important not to fully close the chakras as this would affect the healthy functioning of the physical body.

When the spirit(s) are no longer being perceived

by the child they will usually move on, provided there is no attachment to the property.

So why do children see spirits?

When we are born our strongest sense is the intuitive one, but as we experience this physical dimension we start to rely on the information we receive through our five physical senses: sight, hearing, smell, taste and touch. We can soon 'forget' to use our intuitive ability because our parents and then society condition us to use and rely on information obtained though our five physical senses and our logical reasoning mind. We are brought up to believe that if we cannot see something physically it is not real, and so before very long our attention turns away from non-physical intuition.

I have seen this very clearly with my own children. At two Liam was able to 'see' the spirits that worked with me when I saw healing clients and up until the age of five it was common for Sarah to portray the aura glow around the stick-people she drew instead of putting clothes on them.

I believe that children are born psychically open but that they gradually close down this ability when it is not reinforced. It has been hard enough for me as a grown-up coming to terms with my abilities and people's reactions to them. Rightly or wrongly, Andrew and I have chosen not to consciously develop our children's abilities to see spirit world at this time. Instead we have valued them forming regular friendships with children of their own age

— it can be hard feeling different at any age but particularly so as a child.

Friendships are built on areas of common ground. We are drawn to people who feel the same as us, who share our values. Were Sarah and Liam to feel too 'different' they would have trouble forming friendships with other children. When they are older, if they are curious, then we will see what is possible for them. The abilities are not lost, they are just not paid attention to for a little while.

There are lots of ways that children may reveal their psychic abilities. Seeing spirit world is just one way. Here are some of the other phenomena I have come across over the years.

Children who see auras

This is undoubtedly the most common phenomenon I have witnessed and heard about. There are a great many children around who can see the human energy field — commonly referred to as the aura. The *Magic Eye* pictures that have hidden three-dimensional images within them cause us to focus our eyes differently, and this just happens to be the very same way we need to focus to see auras. If your child is seeing auras it might be worth asking what it is they see and, if they are old enough, to get them to teach you what it is they do with their eyes to see the aura. In time humanity will develop this ability further and this will allow illnesses not only to be diagnosed using this non-invasive method, but also treated before they have manifested on a physical level.

Children who see fairies

Yes, there are children who can and do see fairies. Isn't that wonderful?! I have never had the experience myself and nor have my children but it hasn't been for want of trying.

If your child can see fairies you are very fortunate — it is something I still hope to learn.

Again I encourage you to talk to them about what they experience and let them know that this is a natural ability.

Children with invisible friends

Psychologists take the view that children create invisible friends to express another side of them, or to better express their own needs. More than likely if your child has an invisible friend it is imagined but there are times when children may experience either a spirit-world child or one of their own guides who appears to them at a similar age so they can relate to them better. The difference between the former and the latter is very apparent.

Have you ever known an invisible friend to be from Arcadia? Or be called Medoc? These two names would definitely indicate a guide. If the invisible friend turns up just in time for dessert to get an extra helping, or is responsible for breaking a treasured toy, or putting yoghurt on the cat, they are likely to be imagined.

Both my kids have had both kinds of invisible friends at different times. The best way to handle it is to be curious and notice if they start giving you information a child of their age would not be likely to know.

Imaginary friends are part of growing up. Recent studies have shown that imaginary friends and personified toys are a lot more commonplace than most people realise. Whether they are a girl called Marmalade who walks your child to school on their first day, or invisible kittens like my sister had, they are an extension of your child's play. It has been shown that children with imaginary friends tend to have better verbal skills and social understanding, but if we don't have them — and I didn't — that is fine too.

Remote viewing

One of my nieces, when very young, announced to her mum that, 'Grandma's got a blue car today.'

'No honey, Grandma's car is red,' said Mum. But later that day when Mum was speaking on the phone to Grandma it turned out that Grandma had taken hers in to get repaired and the garage had lent her a blue car for the day. Grandma lived several miles away from the granddaughter and Mum and the child had not left the house all day, so there was no rational explanation for the granddaughter's insight.

This intuitive skill can be highly developed in many young children, with them knowing information that logic tells us they cannot know. It can make it difficult for parents wishing to surprise their child with a birthday present!

Precognition

This is the ability to perceive information about events before they happen, as opposed to merely predicting them based on deductive reasoning or current knowledge. Recently at a show a lady came over to me to say that the weekend before, her ten-year-old daughter had come to her to say that they would be burgled. The daughter, who had never said anything like this before, felt so strongly about this that Mum turned the car around and went back to the house and checked every window with her daughter. The very next day they were burgled while everyone was out. The daughter's precognition had been realised.

Healing

A friend of mine has a four-year-old son who will walk up to her and lay his hands on the place where she is experiencing pain and say, 'Make you better', and he does. Many children have the ability to heal, and just need a gentle nudge in that direction. In our family we have changed through the generations. In my generation when I hurt myself I would go running to Mum and she would lift me onto the kitchen bench and bathe my wounds. With my own children we started to do hands-on healing instead but very soon found they pushed our hands away and held their own hands there instead. It's great when we see them doing what comes naturally and watch as other kids who come to play follow their example, placing their own hands on their cuts and bruises to see if they can make them feel better.

Sensitivity

The old word for 'medium' used to be 'sensitive', and with good reason. To discern the non-physical dimensions you need to be very sensitive as they are more subtle than the physical energies. Sensitive means what it says and sensitive children (and adults) tend to be more emotionally sensitive than others. The benefit is that this gives them empathy for others, and the downside is that other children and adults can easily hurt them.

Many children then defend their sensitivity with a false shell. I have found that rather than have this happen it is better to help the child become more self-aware, to notice what it is they are feeling and why.

Being sensitive in and of itself is not the problem, but being afraid that our feelings will overwhelm or embarrass us, is. Once we can see that our feelings are natural we become less afraid to feel them and more open to being who we truly are.

Sensitive children can also display a series of allergies — to wheat, milk, sugar, chemicals and many other substances. The allergy isn't really a problem. It is their bodies' way of refining their diet and changing their environment so it is more conducive to their spiritual growth. I prefer to see allergies as blessings that guide us in the right direction, rather than something that we need to overcome.

Above all, with any kind of psychic phenomenon children need to know that what they are experiencing is natural. Their experiences, whatever they may be, are signs of the sixth sense that we all have. Accessing this sixth sense can assist us in life; it can help us to understand ourselves better and to communicate with others better. It can help us become a better sister, brother or friend.

Here are some of the things Andrew and I have done with our own children to develop their intuition in a very natural way. First and foremost we have helped our children to be very self-aware. Aware of how they feel within themselves, towards others and towards the earth. We have helped them understand that the feelings that arise within them are caused by a thought and to notice what that thought is — for then they will learn something very important about themselves.

We have played games with them to develop their psychic abilities in a fun way. We have taken turns guessing the colour of a playing card in the car on long journeys. We have imagined ourselves at the place where we are staying before we get there. We have sat in the bush being open to seeing or sensing nature spirits. We have felt how water really feels and noticed how it tastes when we have blessed it. And we have sat under the stars and contemplated our place in this vast universe. There are lots of ways you can help your children stay open in a natural way.

My concerns about sensitive children needing to protect themselves were cleared away a couple of years ago. Sarah, my daughter, has taught me more about protection than I have ever taught her.

A friend of Sarah's came around to play one day and when the child's mother came to collect her the daughter went into the whiny mood she had arrived in. We had not seen the mood the whole day, but now Mum was here it surfaced again.

'Do you know, Lois, you really tire me when you are like this,' complained Mum as she picked up her daughter's scattered belongings.

'You should protect your energy like I do,' said Sarah matter-of-factly.

Lois's mum's mouth fell open, as did mine.

Talking to Sarah later I asked her what she meant. She explained that the first day Lois came to play it had been great and they had had lots of fun, but the second time she started feeling really tired and grumpy like Lois was. So she stopped Lois taking her energy and now everything was fine.

'How did you do that?' I asked curiously.

Sarah shrugged. 'I just decided that I didn't want her to take my energy any more. I still want to play with her.'

There are different ways that we can protect ourselves energetically. The best known is probably to surround yourself with white light. To do this you just imagine yourself in a bubble of white light. Put the bubble of white light all around you and under your feet.

Sarah's way was simply to hold the intent that she didn't want Lois taking her energy and so she couldn't.

We have only very recently started introducing our children to meditation. We started with a candle flame, as kids love candles, and have progressed to a meditation CD. I have been inundated with requests for something for children and so a CD of meditations for children is now available through my website, www.jeanettewilson.com.

After the question about children who see spirits the next most popular question I am asked about children is, what do I think about indigo children?

The term 'indigo children' was coined by the authors of the book *The Indigo Children*, Lee Carroll and Jan Tober. The book describes the characteristics of the new kind of children who have been coming onto the earth for some years.

People seem particularly interested to find out if my own children are indigo children. When answering this question I always start by explaining that I believe that every child is unique, every child is special and needs to be treated as an individual, but if terms such as 'indigo child' or 'crystal child' help us understand and appreciate our children or ourselves better then that can be useful.

As humanity evolves, so the children that are born into each successive generation have a tendency to be more evolved than their parents. This is a generalisation though; it depends on what we have come here to learn and clearly there will be exceptions to this.

Consider your own family — think about those older than you and those younger than you: does anyone stand out as being more or less evolved? Wiser, kinder, more loving?

It is important to remember that as Spirit we are eternal — our spiritual journey never ends, it is like a circle. We are all at different points on the circle, and it honestly doesn't matter where we are on the circle, what matters is that we keep moving. So it isn't really fair to say that one generation is any better than another; we are just learning different things.

My grandmother's life, for example, was very difficult. Her own mother died when she was quite young, leaving her to bring up her younger brothers and sisters. Grandma only learned to read and write later in life after she was married. My grandfather taught her to read in her twenties. My grandparents had four children, and with the help of their older children they scrimped and saved to send my father to university. He was the only member of his family to have the opportunity to go to university and that brought with it its own challenges.

By the time I left school, university was freely available, but I chose not to go. In my generation I can see that we have more choices. Our paths aren't necessarily any easier, there are just different choices available to us, and we have different qualities to meet these challenges. The world I live in is very different from the world my grandmother knew.

The term 'indigo child' is used to describe a particular set of characteristics that are revealing themselves in a generation of human beings. From what I have read about indigo children, they can have clairvoyant and healing abilities. They often behave as though they are royalty. Self-worth is just not an issue; they know who they are and will tell you. Indigo children dislike authority when it is imposed for no logical or rational reason and dislike routines that they can see no logic or reason behind. Indigo children will find fault with existing systems, be it at school, at home or in the workplace. Their questioning can be viewed negatively by others but they can be guided to help reform and improve existing systems. Indigo children can often be misdiagnosed as having Attention Deficit with Hyperactivity Disorder (ADHD) or Attention Deficit Disorder (ADD). Sadly the drug that is prescribed to many children diagnosed with ADHD and ADD is methylphenidate, commonly known as Ritalin. Many people do not realise that the US Drug Enforcement Administration has classified Ritalin as a Schedule II drug, with an equivalent ranking to cocaine. A Schedule II drug is considered to have high potential for misuse. You could say that when Ritalin is administered by a doctor for legitimate medical uses that it is okay, but the drug clearly has a lot of vocal opponents, especially in the US (see Appendix, page 222). At the very least Ritalin is likely to cause the child to lose their psychic abilities and warrior energy.

So are my own children indigo children? No, they are not. But I have to admit, I may well be. Mum always said I needed a maid (I think I still do) and at three years old I had a stand-up argument with my dad in which I told him that I was me and he was him and that he could not make me do anything. At the time he was trying to stop me from banging a drum. I liked the sound of the drum and he didn't. My father was aghast that I should speak to him in such a way, especially when I was so young. I was sent to my room but my dad didn't win the argument because I knew I was right — and I *knew* Dad knew it too. I am so glad I didn't have myself as a child this lifetime.

Seriously, apart from this one incident I was a very well-behaved child, intelligent and kind, but I knew very early in my life that no one could make me do something if I didn't want to. They still can't.

As an adult I have often been described as 'arrogant'. I don't mean to be, but when I can see so clearly what needs to happen in a situation, whether it is genetic engineering or global warming, I get terribly frustrated that people cannot see what I see. Especially when those people are in places of power and should, in my opinion, know better.

Believing we know a thing when we don't does a hell of a lot more damage than admitting we do not know. Aren't we supposed to learn that one as kids? There is a lot that we need to investigate more, such as . . . What really causes cancer? Are the vaccines we inject into our children's bloodstreams really safe and effective? Is putting fluoride, a waste product in the manufacture of fertiliser, in our drinking water really a good thing to do?

We humans can be downright dumb at times — we dump waste underground and we *know* that it is not going to decompose. We also know that the population is increasing so we know we will need to dump more and more waste, and we also know that this earth is not getting any bigger. So why keep dumping stuff in the ground? In fact, why manufacture it anyway? Why not manufacture things that will naturally decompose when they have fulfilled their purpose?

Or even better, make things that last — like they used to?

Enough said. You can see I undoubtedly fit the description of an indigo child, and I still have some serious growing up to do! I can't help it though — I just see through the lies, and I can't go along with what I see because it is not in my nature to pretend I don't know something, to deny my own truth.

Now imagine me at school; imagine lots of kids like me at school. The schools are trying to fill my head with information that *someone in the government thinks I ought to know*. I have to sit exams to show what? Not that I am smart — I am smart enough to know that exams just test memory. That's not what real intelligence is. And those deemed 'smartest' get to have the 'best' jobs as lawyers and doctors and fill their heads with more 'stuff'.

It keeps them away from thinking for a few years. It keeps them from asking the really important questions like 'what on earth is going on here? How come we have food piles in one part of the world and in other parts of the world millions die of starvation?' It keeps them from thinking about how they would *really* like to spend their life.

Then the jobs are so stressful they don't get to enjoy their lives and they stress themselves into an early grave, and that we call *success*!

No wonder so many kids are dropping out of school; no wonder so many are turning to drugs. We live in a crazy world! So crazy a child could see it — but we grown-ups either don't see it or we go along with it because that's what everyone else does.

Yes, I am definitely an indigo child and I *feel* for all those children like me who need a different kind of education. Our children and our grandchildren are the ones who will inherit the consequences of all our actions and inactions. Now more than ever it is essential that we nurture their sensitivity and creativity, so that they can find effective solutions to the challenges we previous generations have created. And that is why I put a lot of time, energy and effort into creating the Eco Schools. I say Eco Schools; there is only one at the moment, but my dream is for more as more people become inspired to do something different for their children and their grandchildren.

I have to channel all this frustration in a positive way! I know there is a better way for us all to live. One that is driven by the pure joy of being alive — not by money or debt or what we fear.

For every problem facing humanity at this time the solution also exists — we just have to be open to seeing it. There are a great many people coming up with creative solutions to the world's problems and I think it is an amazing time to be on the earth, because humanity is changing, and the more you notice the signs, the more you notice the signs.

With any problem in your life, in your community, or in the world, *if you aren't part of the solution you are part of the problem*. If you would like something different it is time to start imagining that — not just changing what you now have but imagining something *completely different*, how you would *love* your life to be. Imagine it and love it into being.

So going back to my children — no, they are not like me. They are gentle, compassionate souls. Incredibly loving, and more like the crystal children that you read about. Crystal children are happy and even-tempered with large eyes that seem to look right into your soul. They may have the occasional tantrum, but you find that they forgive others easily and are very easy-going. They are naturally telepathic and that can get them into trouble. Imagine a group of crystal children sitting an exam within the existing system — they would be accused of cheating! Because they are telepathic they can be slow to speak. Don't let it worry you; if they are loving and cuddly and connect with you, not speaking till later is not a sign of autism, it's the sign of a crystal child.

I am here, like many indigo children, to rock the

cage of the establishment — to challenge how we perceive things and to assist in societal reform. My children, as crystal children, with many others will be reaping the benefit of this reform and bringing in the new age of peace, caring and co-operation. The crystals are the generation who will take us into a safer and more peaceful world. And look at them, look at their wonderful qualities — their sensitivity, gentleness and love: if this is where humanity is heading we truly have nothing to fear.

WALK WITH ME

Walk with me and I'll show you a world
    where food grows freely on trees,
Walk with me and I'll show you a world
    that is free of death and dis-ease.
I'll show you a path,
I'll show you a way,
To help you remember once more,
That you are not what you think,
You are not what you say,
My child, you are so much more.
A world where we share, a world where we
    care, regardless of colour or race.
Where each person's happy to be as they
    are, and the world is a peaceful place.

*So come walk with me and I'll show you
 the way,
You haven't that far to go.
It's a place that you've visited many a day,
It's the place that only you know.
It's the place where you're loving,
The place where you're kind,
The place where you simply can be.
It's inside your heart,
The seat of your soul,
It's the place that you set yourself free
By loving yourself and loving your life,
And trusting that what's meant to be
Will unfold in your life in its own perfect
 way,
And by placing your trust in Me*.*

* God/the divine spark within

Appendix

Ritalin

There have been at least 19 cases of sudden death in children taking methylphenidate (the generic name for the drug, of which Ritalin is a brand name), leading to calls by the Drug Safety and Risk Management Advisory Committee to the US Food and Drug Administration to require the most serious type of health warning on the label, but this advice was rejected (New Scientist, 18 February 2006).

On February 9, 2006, the Drug Safety and Risk Management Advisory Committee voted by a margin of eight to seven to recommend a 'black box' warning describing the cardiovascular risks of stimulant drugs used to treat attention deficit/

hyperactivity disorder (ADHD). On March 22, 2006 the FDA Pediatric Advisory Committee decided that the medications did not need black-box warnings about their risks. The FDA declined to include these black-box warnings upon review. (Source: www.wikipedia.org)

Other websites drawing attention to the possible dangers and side effects of Ritalin include www.adhdfraud.org and www.audiblox2000.com/learning_disabilities/ritalin.htm